Through Another's Eyes

Lowell A. King

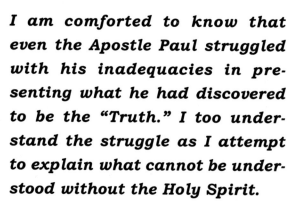

I am comforted to know that even the Apostle Paul struggled with his inadequacies in presenting what he had discovered to be the "Truth." I too understand the struggle as I attempt to explain what cannot be understood without the Holy Spirit.

—Lowell King

When I came to you, brothers, I did not come with eloquence or superior wisdom as I proclaimed to you the testimony about God. For I resolved to know nothing while I was with you except Jesus Christ and him crucified. I came to you in weakness and fear, and with much trembling. My message and my preaching were not with wise and persuasive words, but with a demonstration of the Spirit's power, so that your faith might not rest on men's wisdom, but on God's power. (1 Corinthians 2:1-5, NIV 1985)

Dedication and Acknowledgements

I, Lowell King, want to dedicate this book to the Holy Spirit. Without him, not even one page could have been written.

I would also like to acknowledge my wife, Cecilia, my sons, Ralph and Troy, my editor, Christina Miller of Mentor's Pen Editorial Services, Donna Nullmeyer, who helped with transcription, and my friends Wayne and Ida Lindeman, Greg and Sandy Smolin, Barry and Sylvia Vorpahl, Tom and Nancy Hird, Marion Scharfe, Kathy Weber, and last but not least, Sehra Gaschani.

Without the support, encouragement, and prayers of my family and friends, this book never would have been written.

Regarding Cover of the Book

The book cover is a movie clip from the film, "The Lazarus Phenomenon", Produced by, W.Johan Sturm.

The photo shows the "Rich Man" in the parable Jesus spoke about in Luke 16:19-31.

The "Rich Man" is suffering in hell, begging Abraham to allow Lazarus to come to him and put a drop of cold water on his tongue.

Abraham explains that there is a great chasm between them that prevents Lazarus from coming to comfort this poor suffering soul.

A special thank you to W. Johan Sturm for providing this photo and granting permission to use it in the production of this book.

Chapter One

———⟊———

Although my bed was the most comfortable that money could buy, I couldn't sleep.

As always for the past ten years, my mind was in torment over the possible consequences of my bad and even unethical business decisions. But worse than that, I feared my nightmare of the night before would return.

God, must I relive that childhood event for the rest of my life? The recurring dream hadn't stopped after all this time, so why did I expect a miracle now? I wished it had never happened, but it had. In the dream and in my past, my best friend, Reuben, and I were in competition. We were climbing a tree in the middle of town, all the neighborhood children watching. Reuben was a year older and slightly taller and stronger—always the best at everything we did. This day I was determined to challenge Reuben and reach the top of the tree faster and higher than we'd ever done before.

As Reuben ascended, I was right behind him, scrambling up the side of the opposite tree. Pride and foolishness and surging pulses drove us both as we climbed higher and higher. Finally, I was afraid to go higher, but Rueben reached for a too-skinny branch.

"Reuben, don't try it!"

Before the words were out of my mouth, Reuben's little branch broke, and Reuben freefell through the air. With a thud, he reached the ground.

As I clambered down my tree, I could hear Rueben gasping for air and moaning. I rushed to his side, and the groaning got louder. His neck wrangled to a grotesque angle, he gripped me with the only part of his body he could move—his eyes.

I ran for his parents, but when we returned, Reuben told us in a cold voice that he couldn't move. In my dream, I know what I didn't know when the accident happened: Reuben would never move again.

His mother screamed at me. "I told you not to climb those trees. If you hadn't taunted him, he would have obeyed me. This is your fault!"

How would his life have been different if I had not challenged him on that day? How would mine?

I was grieved that over the years I have not taken time to visit Reuben. I would never admit this to anyone but God, but I was afraid to visit him for fear of seeing blame in his eyes. There was nothing I could say. But the worst thing was the fact that I was more concerned about myself than I was about my friend.

My name is Demas. I am a lifelong resident of the city of Capernaum in the nation of Israel. I was born and raised in this city. My father was a farmer and raised livestock here, a successful businessman and a good family man.

The story I'm about to tell you occurred 2000 years ago. It's the story of my life, my decisions, and their consequences. It's also the story of my neglect of the most important responsibilities of my life: those of father and husband.

I'm an investment broker, and this day, when my story starts, I was preparing for a long trip to Jerusalem to visit some high-ranking Roman clients. Unfortunately, my job that day was to tell them that the investments I made on their behalf had failed. These men were powerful and held the fate of my life in their hands. It was anybody's guess whether I would spend that night in my lavish home or in a cold jail cell—or worse.

There were two sets of laws in Israel in that day: one for Israeli people, among our own community, and another for the nation of Israel, upheld by the Roman government. Israel was held in slavery and any violation of the law by an Israeli citizen against a Roman citizen had drastic consequences.

I wish I could say I had more integrity in my home life than I had in my business life. I'm married to a wonderful woman, Goldie, and we have two children, my then-nine-year-old son Herschel and seven-year-old Judith. On the outside, I looked like a good example—except for my business practices. My family was active in the Temple, and I was a large contributor. Most people saw our family as a model family in the community. But at home, I was a tyrant with radical mood swings and little patience with my wife and children. I constantly made unreasonable demands on them.

And for that, I am sorry.

On this fateful day that will change my life forever, my wife was busy sewing a special pocket in the hem of my cloak so I could hide most of the money I would take with me on the trip. Our servants scurried around, making preparations. My most trusted servant, Joseph, was packing my donkeys. And while they did the work of packing, I could think only of the consequences I might face. What was I going to say when I met my clients? The thought of prison paralyzed my mind. A conviction would put me out of business. We would lose all we had acquired, and it would be the end of our grand lifestyle.

As I left that morning, my family tried to say goodbye to me, standing outside our home, hoping I would embrace them and give them a kiss goodbye. But I didn't take the time to acknowledge their expression of love and concern or give them an affectionate farewell. Instead, I walked away after giving them a long list of things I wanted them to accomplish in my absence.

My servant Joseph was standing by the donkeys. Joseph and I had become very good friends over the years. Although he was a servant, he was educated and intelligent and was the only man in the household I felt I could sit down and talk with.

Joseph had been watching with a keen eye and listening with a sharp ear when I approached him. He said, "Master Demas, your family loves you and wants some of your attention."

I knew he was right, but I wasn't going to acknowledge the comments of a servant, friend or no friend. "Remember who you are, Joseph." I walked away with my donkeys in tow.

Initially, the business I had started was unsuccessful because of my lack of knowledge and experience. One day, I heard about a man named Eli, who had been in the same business I was trying to enter into. Age had taken its toll on Eli, giving him arthritis and a bad hip that forced him to retire on his limited savings. He was almost destitute and in need of some kind of employment.

When I heard about Eli, I realized I could learn from him and combine his knowledge and abilities with my negotiating skills and my physical ability to travel. We could form a very viable partnership.

Eli took me up on that opportunity, and over the years, our business grew and became increasingly successful. As I became more competent, I also became more of a tyrant, at work as well as at home. I took advantage of him and made unreasonable demands, knowing he had no choice but to stay in the partnership.

As I entered our place of business, I greeted him with a list of demands I wanted fulfilled while I was gone. But for the first time, he challenged me. I had to remind him who was in control.

"You know, Eli," I said, "I'm sure there are many young men who could do the same job you're doing, would work for less, and would possibly take some of my responsibility so I wouldn't have to work so hard."

And he looked at me and said, "Work so hard? All you do is go off on these long trips and enjoy fine meals and fine wines, having a good time while I'm here working."

"Oh, so that's the problem! You're jealous of what I do, in spite of the fact you're unable to do it yourself. I am the one who brings in the clients. I provide the business income. Maybe I should find one of those men and send you on your way."

A sheen formed on his brow. "I didn't say I wanted you to do that."

I knew Eli couldn't live on his meager savings, so he had no choice but to stay in the partnership and basically be my servant. No matter what, I could never allow him to realize how much I depended on his experience.

He pulled a cloth from his pocket and wiped his face. "I'm sorry, Demas. Please don't do that."

I realized I'd pushed him about as far as I could that day, so I changed the subject and finished the details of the items I wanted him to accomplish while I was gone. Before I left the office that day, I told Eli I would be spending the evening in town. He knew where I'd be. I instructed him not to divulge my whereabouts to anyone, but if he needed me in case of an emergency, he knew where to find me.

It was my routine to spend the night in town before I left on a trip. A young woman named Rahab would be my companion for the evening. Many of the men in town were familiar with Rahab and used her services. I'm sure many of the wives knew their husbands were spending time with her, but it was an accepted practice that no one talked about.

As I left the office that day, I could tell I had pushed Eli beyond his limit. He was a mild-mannered person with high ethical and moral standards. He was a believer in God, which was something I did not claim to be, in spite of my weekly appearance at Temple. He was also especially frustrated with me because of my immoral activities and my lack of business ethics. But he didn't say much about it, probably because he was afraid of my response.

I led my donkeys across town and left them with the stable master near my destination. I gave him instructions to feed and water and brush down my donkeys and told him I would come back early the next morning.

Although I was ruthless in my business dealings and disrespectful of my wife and children, I was gentle with my animals. I couldn't make my journeys without the donkeys. I treated them with tender, loving care.

After leaving the donkeys, I traveled down a side street, looking over my shoulder to make sure no one I knew was around. I made a quick right turn down an alley and scaled up the familiar stairway. It was a conveniently secluded second-story residence.

Rahab wasn't her real name. She was a young girl, very beautiful, orphaned as a child and raised by abusive family members. Like many women in her situation, she entered the business in order to escape that home and provide for herself. At least, so she said.

As I came up the stairs, the door opened. Rahab greeted me with a slight smile. "Spending the night, Demas?"

"Yes, and leaving first thing in the morning." I paused. "If you're not already occupied."

She held out her hand. "If you have the money, I have the time."

I knew what she meant when she held out her hand. So I paid her the fee and went in.

Later I found out that, back at the business, Eli was working on the list I had given to him. One of his friends, Hyam, stopped by to chat with him during his morning break. It was not uncommon for Hyam to come by. He had been friends with Eli for many years. He was older than Eli and had already reached retirement and was financially secure. The two would talk about old times and the things they had accomplished throughout their lives. I didn't ever complain about Hyam visiting the business because I knew there were times when Eli was there by himself with nothing to do, and it was one way of allowing him some freedom I knew he enjoyed.

I later learned from an eavesdropper that when Hyam arrived in the morning, Eli complained to him about the conversation we'd had that morning.

"The world would be better off without him," Hyam said.

Eli hated violence and struggled with the idea of harming anyone, even someone who had harmed him as I had done earlier in the morning. Finally, Hyam convinced him that if I didn't exist anymore, he would have control of the business. Hyam then argued that even Goldie and the children would be better off without me because of my immoral lifestyle and the way I treated them.

Eli was not completely convinced he should be part of a murder plot, but he did agree to speak to a small group of mercenaries, friends of Hyam's, who had just arrived in town. These mercenaries hated the Roman citizens and anyone who did business with the Romans, which included me. They also hated the tax collectors, whom they knew had sold their souls to the Roman government and exploited the people of Israel. Some of my best clients were tax collectors. They were rich, and I didn't care where their money came from. But I always knew my involvement with them made me a target for the Romans' violence.

After a meeting with the mercenaries in the afternoon, everyone agreed they would take my life the next morning when I left town on my journey to Jerusalem. I, of course, was completely oblivious to the arranged plan, and my evening was spent as usual, with Rahab.

The mercenaries set up camp about four miles out of town. They dug a shallow grave in preparation for my body.

The next morning, I said my goodbyes to Rahab, and I made my way back to the stable. My donkeys were all prepared for me, and I left town early that morning.

I remember going down a well-traveled path leading toward Jerusalem. As I walked along the trail, I thought about my wealth and my power. I was glad I had the protection of the Roman government as well as the religious leaders in town. I believed I was above ever being assaulted by anyone because everybody knew who I was. They knew I had friends in high places throughout Israel. I had become well known throughout the whole nation and respected by many people. But I underestimated the hatred people had toward me because of my affiliation with the tax collectors and the Roman government. That alliance was about to cost me more than I ever dreamed.

Chapter Two

A few hours later, two men approached me on the road leading from Capernaum. Both of them led donkeys and looked like travelers coming toward the town I'd just left. Getting closer, the first man smiled and said, "Good morning," but the crescent-shaped scar on his cheek and the hardness of his eyes made me wary that this morning might not turn out to be good at all.

As we met in the road, he stopped and peered at me through narrowed eyes. "How far to Capernaum?"

I kept walking, my instincts telling me to be careful, and called over my shoulder, "Three and a half or four miles."

As I was turning to keep him within my vision, I heard fast footsteps from the other direction. Before I could respond, the second man raised a heavy club and swung. I dodged the blow but he was faster, and the impact dropped me to my knees.

With blood in my eyes and pain that made me swear my head was split in two, I took a swing at the figure that grew dimmer by the second. Then the second man must have joined the beating as I felt hard punches to my face and gut.

Unable to see and becoming too weak with pain to defend myself, I covered my head with my hands, but they continued to hit me over and over. I must have gone into shock because at some point, although the beating continued, the pain was gone.

Then they were dragging me by my heels. I wanted to get up and break free to defend myself, but there was no fight left in me. I was in complete submission and at the mercy of my aggressors.

As we approached the shallow grave, they threw me in, face down, burying me alive.

I could still hear them talking as they piled rocks on me. One landed on my right leg, just below my knee. There was a loud cracking noise as my leg broke, and I screamed out in pain.

Alerted that I was still alive, one of the men plunged a dagger into my back, miraculously missing my major organs. The last thing I remember was a panicked voice saying, "Someone's coming. Let's get out of here."

One of the men dropped a large stone on the back of my skull, clearly hoping to crush it. From that point on, everything was black.

I have no idea how long the darkness lasted, but in time I found myself standing in a beautiful garden. The colors were amazing, and it seemed as though my eyes were seeing things differently than ever before. Colors and objects jumped out at me like stars in the sky on a clear night. All my senses seemed enhanced. I don't remember ever in my lifetime looking at a tree or plant and thinking about its beauty, but for some reason, things were now different. And the pain from my beating was gone.

I turned to see a magnificent city sitting on a hill. Light radiated from that city, enhancing the beauty surrounding it, and its walls were like jasper, clear as crystal. A rainbow surrounded it, and thunder rumbled after flashes of lightening with the voices of a multitude singing over and over, "Hallelujah."

I was drawn toward the city. The closer I walked toward the light, the more profound my sense of joy and beauty grew.

Finally, I stopped, because I knew if I took one more step, I wouldn't be able to bear the sensations I was experiencing. I sat down on a nearby rock and soaked in everything around me.

As I tried to analyze this joy, I realized it was different from any I had experienced in my life. The things that had brought me joy in the past were both temporary and temporal. But this present joy was on the inside, continually intensifying.

All the trees and plants around me were in bloom, pruned perfectly. There were no weeds, and the trees were filled with songbirds singing together in harmony. They all faced the city, serenading the light as if in gratitude.

A river flowed from a glassy sea in front of the city and ran through the garden. The water was crystal-clear, sparkling like diamonds as it reflected the city.

The light was exceptionally bright but didn't hurt my eyes. In fact, it was hard not to look at it. There was no hint of darkness. Everything was revealed, nothing hidden.

At the base of one of the trees just ahead of me, a doe stood over a reclining lion. The doe's fawn lay snuggled against the lion's side.

At first, I thought the lion was about to devour the fawn, but then I realized they were simply snuggling together for a nap. I sensed no fear of the lion, and I didn't understand. I had always been afraid of any kind of wild beast, especially those that might consider me a meal. Something inside told me there was nothing to fear.

All of a sudden, my mind flashed back to the struggle that seemed to have occurred just moments before. I touched my head where the rock had hit my skull. I realized I was standing on the leg I knew had been broken, and yet there was no pain.

But wait—how could my wounds heal so quickly, and where was I? Moments ago, I was being buried alive. I could still feel the weight of the stones being piled on top of me.

What kind of place was this? How did I get here? Was I dead? Was this what happens when you die, or was it a dream? If it was, I didn't want to wake up and find myself buried under three feet of rock.

Just about that time, I heard a voice behind me say, "No, Demas, this is not a dream. You are now in Paradise."

I spun toward the voice. "Who are you?"

"I am your guide. You must follow me. I will explain everything, and all your questions will be answered shortly."

I reluctantly took his hand, and as we walked away from the light, the joy drained out of me. "But I don't want to go this way. I want to go toward the light."

The guide said, "Follow me, and you'll soon have answers to all your questions."

Then we were airborne, flying across a great chasm, and we landed on what the guide called the Other Side. From that viewpoint, I could still see Paradise. I could still hear the sounds of laughter and singing. I could see the great light, but the light did not penetrate the darkness where I now stood.

It wasn't that the light was unable to reach the Other Side; it was as if the light was reserved for those in Paradise. Those on the Other Side were restricted from enjoying its pleasure.

My joyful feeling was gone, replaced by emptiness and fear, apprehension and hopelessness. "Where have you taken me?"

"To your future home, Demas."

"I don't want to be here. I want to go back to where I started."

"This is your future home. This is the home you will receive as a result of decisions you made during your time on earth. This will be your chosen home for eternity."

This couldn't be happening. "I didn't choose this place."

"No, but you chose not to be part of God's kingdom. That side is called Paradise. You rejected all God had to offer, choosing the world instead. This new home is the consequence of your decisions. During the time you will spend here, you will remember the many attempts God made to call you into his family. Your being here is not his choice. This is not what he wants for you. But Paradise is the place for those who choose to live with God and his son, Jesus, and be part of his family."

This had to be a bad dream. I just wanted to wake up. "Can I go back and have a second chance? Please, tell me what I can do."

"I can do only what I've been called to do. My job is to bring you here and leave you. I must go now and escort others."

I grabbed at his sleeve. "You can't just leave me here. How will I survive?"

"You will wish you could die, but there's no death here. There's only eternal life. This is the life you chose—a life in which you will be separated from God the Father and his Son."

And with that, he disappeared.

It was extremely dark where I was standing. The light from the city in Paradise seemed to reach only the edge of the chasm. I walked toward the edge to see if there was just enough light to look down. The chasm appeared to have no bottom. As far as I could see, there was only blackness with a little white speck at the bottom.

I picked up a rock and threw it into the chasm to see how deep it was, but the rock bounced back.

I could see and hear the sounds from Paradise, but an invisible barrier prevented anything from crossing the chasm. No one could cross the divide or even kill himself by throwing himself into it. Whatever was to come, I was going to have to go through it. There was no way to turn back.

I began to think about the choices I had made that led me to this awful place. My heart broken, I fell to my knees and wept—alone.

Chapter Three

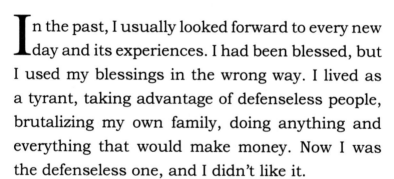

In the past, I usually looked forward to every new day and its experiences. I had been blessed, but I used my blessings in the wrong way. I lived as a tyrant, taking advantage of defenseless people, brutalizing my own family, doing anything and everything that would make money. Now I was the defenseless one, and I didn't like it.

My wrong choices had come back to haunt me. On the Other Side, there were no choices. There was no time here. There were no clocks, there was no daytime, only nighttime and eternity. No rest, no peace, no sleep, no place to hide, no comfort, no joy—nothing to look forward to. Just pain, fear, misery, and constant harassment from the evil ones.

The people on the Other Side were human souls in indestructible bodies that were a curse to those who wished to die but couldn't.

Suddenly, I realized I was not alone. I was surrounded by a multitude of people. The number was so large, it would have taken forever to count even a small portion of them. I looked for familiar faces but found none. It seemed that with so many people, I should find somebody I knew, but I didn't. And when I looked into the eyes of those around me, and I saw nothing but emptiness, fear, and hopelessness. It seemed strange to be in the presence of so many people and yet feel so lonely.

There was no communication between the residents of the Other Side— only the sound of moaning and crying. Men and women with no hope, nothing to look forward to. I talked to several people, but no one would answer me. They just turned away. Maybe they were afraid of me or didn't speak my language. I had so many unanswered questions, I felt paralyzed with fear and confusion.

As I walked past a stone wall, I noticed a wide opening on the left side. People seemed to be backing up to get out of the way of something. And then, for the first time, I saw a demon. He was one of the many who constantly harassed and tormented all the residents of the Other Side. The demons were servants of the fallen angels who had been restricted to the Other Side. The fallen angels and demons all served the self-proclaimed king of the Other Side—Lucifer, Satan, the devil.

The demons spent most of their time on their hands and knees. They were much larger than humans and had no trouble overpowering them. The demons were allowed to inflict great pain and suffering, both emotional and physical. But they could not kill anyone, since there is no death on the Other Side.

I was standing behind this demon and couldn't see his face, but I didn't need to. I knew it had to be frightening because of the terror on the faces of those who were looking directly at him. They would cast their eyes down, but the demon would demand they look at him. This demon was special, and I was about to find out why.

Then the demon spun and looked at me, directly into my eyes. His smile sent chills down my back. I had never seen such a horrible sight, alive or dead.

Then the demon said, "Oh, yes, Demas. I heard you had arrived. My name is Aggravate. You have been personally assigned to me. I am your master. And in time, you will understand what that means. Remember my name. Before I'm through with you, you'll understand why my master calls me Aggravate."

I was unable to move or speak. And then I realized Aggravate was the only being who had spoken to me since I arrived. Maybe Aggravate would know the answers to my questions. "How do you know me?"

"You didn't realize it, but I have been your companion for a long time. You just didn't sense my presence. Over the years, you have been one of my favorite projects because your greed and self-centeredness made you easy to control."

Repulsed, I looked away, but Aggravate demanded that I look back into his face.

"Where am I, and how long do I have to stay here?"

"This is your new home, the home you chose, Demas."

"I didn't choose this place. You sound like the guide."

Aggravate grabbed me by the throat and pulled me to his face. "This is your new home, and I am your master. Get used to it. You will be here until your final day of judgment. Then you'll leave, but you'll wish you could come back. The place you are going will provide, shall we say, new experiences. Then you will consider this place Paradise."

"What are you talking about? Where will I be going?"

"To the bottom of the chasm."

"The bottom?" I looked down into it. "But there isn't a bottom."

"Yes, there is, and you'll see it sooner than you want to. I know because I've seen it, and I know what we will all experience when we get there."

"What do you mean?"

"Your reward is waiting for you there."

"What reward?"

"Your punishment has already been determined. It's not about what you will receive. It's about when you will receive it. Until then, you'll live each moment in fear. The question will never leave your mind: How long will it be? You'll long for the judgment so you can get it over with, but it will never be over."

But I didn't deserve these things. Many people were worse than I was. And I'd done many good things along with the bad. Everyone knew I gave substantial amounts of money to the Temple, and I helped the poor. Most of the time, I tried to do the right thing. I even studied Moses and the Prophets, and I could quote some of the commandments. I didn't belong here at all.

I walked toward the edge of the chasm and looked across to the light. I could see the Heavenly City and the beautiful garden areas and the sparkling river. I longed to feel the love and peace and joy I experienced when I first was in the light. Maybe I would have been better off if I had never seen Paradise, didn't have this constant reminder of what could have been.

As I stood on the edge of the chasm, some new arrivals came in. I began to guess whether they would be escorted to where we were on the Other Side or if they would get to go to the Heavenly City. Watching the joy and amazement of the new citizens was extremely painful because it brought back the memories of what I had experienced when I first arrived.

I felt great compassion for those who arrived on the Other Side. It didn't take me long to understand why no one talked to me when I first got there. I did the same thing to the newcomers that had been done to me. After all, what could I say? Nothing would encourage them. And because there was nothing good to say, no one spoke. Everyone knew the new ones would find out how bad things were soon enough. Soon they would discover their fate. Those of us residing there were so absorbed contemplating our fate that we rarely considered others, even family members who might be arriving. We were all consumed by our own condition.

Some of the new arrivals tried to establish liaisons with the demons in hopes of better treatment. The demons loved this because they knew that making a deal with the devil was an expression of the highest fear. The newcomers didn't understand how much pleasure the demons received from seeing humans suffer. Sometimes they would go along with this idea of a mutual friendship because they knew the weakest among the newcomers would believe them, and then when they found out they were being taken advantage of by the demons, their distress was even greater than those who had avoided being deceived.

And these demons hated us. Humans were made in God's image, and because the demons hated God, they also hated all humans. There was no place for us to hide. We could do nothing to avoid them, and they would do anything they could to see us ravaged in fear and hopelessness.

After a while, I noticed Abraham and Lazarus walking through the garden in Paradise. They sat by the bank of the Sparkling River then knelt to take a cool, refreshing drink. I wondered what the river water tasted like. I thought back to a time when I was a child and our family was traveling. On one of those summer days, I disrobed and jumped into the cool and refreshing water of the

Jordan River. I knew the water in the Sparkling River would be even more refreshing and taste even better. Muddy in spring, the Jordan was never clear and sparkling like the river in Paradise.

I called out, "Father Abraham, have pity on me and send Lazarus to dip his finger in the river and put a drop of water on my tongue to cool my body. I am in great agony."

"Son, in your lifetime, you received all the good things and Lazarus received only the bad things," Abraham said. "Now he is where he belongs, and you are in the place you chose. There's a great chasm between us that keeps us from crossing over. We can't help you." Then they walked away from me toward the Heavenly City.

I cried out, over and over again, "Have pity on me! Have pity on me!"

But there was no response.

One last time, I screamed at the top of my lungs, "Have pity on me!"

And a voice came back. "Silence! Be still."

The voice came from behind me, and there was light for the first time since I had arrived on the Other Side. The light temporarily blinded the entire population of the Other Side, and I heard a loud voice speak with great authority. Every word he spoke made the ground shake, and I said, "Yes, Lord, who are you?"

He said, "I am the Heavenly Father. I am the I Am. I am the Great One."

I fell on my face, completely blinded and humbled in the presence of the Heavenly Father. There was silence for a few minutes, then finally I realized this might be my only opportunity to talk to the Heavenly Father. So I asked if I could present a question.

And he said, "Yes, my son."

I drew a trembling breath. "Why am I here in this place of torment? I thought you were a great God of mercy and love. Why must I suffer this way?"

"I am the source of all love. I have loved you and reached out to you over and over again, but you rejected me. You broke my heart, time and time again. We could have done a lot together, if you had only listened. But you chose not to spend time with me, and you rejected my love, my companionship. I asked very little from you, Demas, but even the small things I requested, you rejected. I asked you to put your faith and trust in me, but you chose to trust gold and silver and the things of the world. You chose your gold over me, and now you are here and your gold is in the hands of others. Your gold is worthless here, and you have nothing you cherished the most. You chose the things you could lose over the one thing you can never lose. There are only two places a person can spend eternity: either with me or without me. This is the place of wrong choices!"

"But I didn't know! If I had known, I would have chosen to be with you. Can't you give me another chance?"

He said, "Don't make excuses, Demas. You know full well the number of times I tried to reach you. From the time you were born, I wrote on your heart the difference between right and wrong, and you chose to do what you pleased. You have no one to blame but yourself."

"Yes, Lord. You are correct." I knew He was right. "I have sinned greatly against you, and for that I am truly sorry. I am not worthy to be in your presence or worthy of this conversation."

"I can see the words coming from your heart. Many others here on the Other Side have expressed the same regret. This does not change their destiny. You chose to reject me. Others chose to live in a way that was pleasing to me, to glorify my name. They put their trust in me. They loved me with all their hearts, and they obeyed me. I am a just God, and justice must prevail."

"Then I beg you to allow me to return home. I have a wife and children and friends and family. Please allow me the opportunity to convince them to change their lives."

"They have not listened to Moses and the Prophets. Why would they listen to you more than those I have sent before you?"

I gathered all the courage I had left. "If you give me the opportunity, I could do what even the great prophets couldn't do. You created me. You know my talents and skills. You blessed me with the ability to persuade people, and you can see I am sincere in my desire to prevent anyone from being separated from you. And I know you do not want anyone to perish. You want all to be saved."

And God said, "Yes, I want everyone to be a part of my family. But I am not convinced about your skills. Human beings are selfish and self-centered and unforgiving, just like you."

"Yes, just like me. But I'm a new person now, and my newfound knowledge, combined with my old skills, would enable me to succeed where others have failed."

Then the Lord said, "I have sent my Son as an ambassador to reach the world. I love my creation, and it is my desire that none should perish. My Son will take a new message to the world—a new covenant. Those who listen and accept my Son will be granted eternal life, and they will become part of my heavenly family.

"As for you, Demas, you are not dead. This is merely a vision of what is to come for both you and all who reject my love. You are going to return to the place you were before your visit to the Other Side. When you return, I will reveal my Son to you. Listen to him. He will speak the truth. Every word he speaks will come from me. When the world has seen my Son, they will see me. He and I are one. As time goes by, you will begin to understand my reasons for allowing you to see into the future. I will be watching to see if this experience will change your life and to see if you can accomplish the goals you have set for yourself.

"Demas, part of your responsibility will be to convince others to listen to my Son and make his instructions part of their lives. If you do these things and they put their trust and confidence in my Son, then they will be saved."

I said, "Thank you, Father. I will not let you down. When can I begin?"

And the Lord said, "Not so fast. You'll have some important rules to obey. If, for any reason, you break any of these rules, you will find yourself a permanent resident of this place of suffering. There will be no second chances."

"Yes, Lord, I understand. I never want to see this place again except from the Paradise side."

Then the Father said, "I want you to tell the people that I prepared hell not for humans, but for Satan and his fallen angels. The only reason humans find themselves here, on the Other Side, is because they have rejected me and the place I prepared for them, the Heavenly City. The choice to be on the Other Side was made by you, not by me."

"I'll tell them."

"First, I will restore your health, but not your wealth. Do you agree?"

And I said, "Yes."

"My Son knows who you are. I will send a sign to reveal to you who he is.

You'll long to be near him, but you may not speak to him or to any of his chosen ones except the one you already know, who he will choose at a later time. When he speaks to you, then you may speak to him. Do you understand?"

I said, "Not exactly, but I know these things will be revealed to me in time."

"There will come a time when you will give up what you cannot keep for what you do not have."

"I'm not sure I understand, Lord."

"You will when the time comes. You will not be allowed to raise your hand to defend my son or comfort him in any way. The days you will be allowed to remain on earth have already been determined. You will not be told the number of days you have to complete your task or when your time on earth will end. You will be the one to make the choice about how your life will end. This you will understand when it occurs.

"Because of some of your unscrupulous business dealings involving Roman citizens and investors, the Roman authorities in Jerusalem have issued a warrant for your arrest. The charges against you are false, but you must remember you will be in danger any time you visit the city of Jerusalem. Do you understand?"

I said, "Yes."

"Now, if you violate any of these rules, our agreement will terminate and you will be in jeopardy of spending eternity in this place of eternal punishment."

Chapter Four

Instantly, I found myself back in the shallow grave. I heard a voice say, "Are you alive?"

All I could do was groan. The traveler who frightened off my would-be murderers then began tossing away the stones piled on top of me.

As the traveler tried to move me, my whole body hurt. My head had been hit hard with the clubs, and the last blow from the stone caused me to drift in and out of consciousness. I could move my shoulders slightly, but that caused pain in my broken arm. My ribs hurt so bad I could hardly breathe, my right leg was definitely broken, and I was bleeding from the stab wound in my back.

The traveler, who was on his way to Jerusalem, said he was from Bethsaida. We had never met before this day, but I was glad he had come along when he did.

I don't remember much after that until I woke up in a small inn somewhere between Capernaum and Jerusalem. There the innkeeper said I had been sleeping several days. He gave me a small bowl of soup—the first nourishment I'd had since the ordeal.

This was going to be a slow and painful process. But at least I was alive and not a resident of the Other Side. Now I needed to focus on recovery so I could get started. I didn't know how much time I had to complete the goals God gave me. But I was hopeful—in fact, I was convinced—that if I changed enough people's minds about how they should live, God would be generous and reward me in some way. The best gift he could give me was to make sure I never became a resident of the Other Side.

I had a heavy responsibility, being the only person God had ever allowed to experience a vision of the Other Side. I was sure that, unless I was successful, many of my friends and relatives would discover their eternal destiny and be brokenhearted as I was when I saw the reality of the Other Side.

After a three-month recovery, I began my journey along the Jordan River toward home. Up ahead, I saw a large crowd of people gathered around a man standing waist-deep in the water. He was saying something, but I couldn't quite hear or understand it.

Getting closer, I saw the man was burly-looking with unfashionably long hair. He shouted at the crowd, "Repent! The kingdom of God is drawing near! God has made provision for those who will admit their sins and return to him and seek to understand his teachings. If you ask forgiveness, repent, and be baptized, you will be added to God's family. Then, and only then, will you be assured of inheriting the Kingdom of God in heaven."

I realized this was the same message God instructed me to give the people. I was anxious to hear more from this man.

He hadn't mentioned anything about good works or helping the poor or giving money to the Temple. If it were this easy, only a fool would refuse to do what this man suggested.

As I moved closer to the crowd, I had to strain to hear him. I asked someone in the crowd, "What is this man's name?"

The man who heard my question responded, "They call him John the Baptist. He's a prophet. The Temple leaders don't like him because he calls them vipers and hypocrites. They're looking for a reason to arrest him, but the people love him because they know his message is from God."

A long line of people waited to be baptized by John. A simple dipping in the river seemed to bring about change. They seemed happy. I couldn't help but wonder what was really happening. "Why do these people seem so happy?"

Another person turned and said, "They're rejecting the way they used to live and committing their lives to God."

Another man who was watching said, "I was already baptized. I asked God's forgiveness and I know He has forgiven me. I feel clean inside and outside. I believe it's some kind of miracle. The burden of sin has been lifted from my shoulders. I feel like a new person—I am free."

As I waited, I studied the people in the line and those watching along the riverbank. It was easy to identify those who approved what John was doing and those who didn't. As I waited, I noticed one young man in line ahead of me. He was about thirty years old. He did not speak to anyone, and there was nothing special about his looks, but for some reason I felt drawn to him and wanted to know who he was.

Looking him over, I wondered why he intrigued me so. Dressed like a common worker, he was obviously not a man of wealth. What could I possibly gain by meeting him? I had always been drawn to people who flaunted their wealth by the way they dressed. People of status and influence—they were always potential clients, people I had a lot in common with and could communicate with. Still, for some reason, this unknown young man interested me.

I was about ten feet away when he stepped forward to be baptized. John the Baptist said, "I need to be baptized by you."

What did he mean by that?

The young man replied, "Let it be so for now, for it is proper for us to do this to fulfill all righteousness."

Now I was really confused.

John consented and baptized the young man.

While I pondered these things, a white dove flew down and perched on the young man's shoulder. Then a voice came from above, the same voice I'd heard in my vision of the Other Side. "This is my Son, in whom I am well pleased."

I looked skyward and then turned and saw John looking up also. Then the young man looked directly at me, and a strange feeling came over me. His eyes spoke volumes of love and compassion.

They did not seem to contain any condemnation, only love and acceptance.

I've heard it said that the eyes are the windows of the soul. His eyes seemed somehow to touch the deepest part of my being.

I sensed that my every thought, both good and evil, had been revealed. I could hide nothing from his deep, piercing eyes. The experience was both intimidating and refreshing. For some reason, I sensed the Son of God and I would be meeting again in the near future. When the time came, I would have to be open and honest with him. God promised he would send a sign, and now I knew this young man was the Son of God. And I understood why I felt drawn to him.

"Did you hear that?" I said to those around me. "That man is the Son of God."

"What man?" someone said.

"The man who was just baptized."

Some of the people seemed confused. Others just ignored me.

I looked back, and I could tell that John had also heard what God the Father had said. But for some reason, only the three of us heard the voice from above.

The young man walked away and did not turn back. He appeared to be on a mission. Nothing was going to stop him.

I began to ask those in the crowd nearby if they knew him.

One lady stepped forward. "I know who he is. His mother's name is Mary, and his father is Joseph. They live in the town where I live, Nazareth. He's a carpenter. His name is Jesus."

Just as the Father had promised, he had sent a sign. Now I had seen the Son, and I knew his name was Jesus. I knew I'd never forget his eyes and how I felt when he looked at me.

I watched as Jesus walked away by himself, plainly dressed. It seemed inappropriate for the Son of God to be dressed this way. Why didn't he have an entourage, an audience, armed guards? It didn't make sense.

I remembered the voice I heard on the Other Side, the same voice that said, "This is my Son, with whom I am well pleased." It was the voice of God the Father.

This meeting with Jesus would not be my last. The Father promised we would see each other again. And I knew that at some point, Jesus would speak to me. I knew I had to be patient and wait for that moment. More than anything, I wanted to follow Jesus right now, but something told me it was not the right time.

I didn't know it at the time, but Jesus was on his way to be tempted by the devil. Jesus would fast and pray for forty days. Then at his weakest moment, the self-proclaimed king of the Other Side would attempt in every way to break him through every temptation known to man.

Satan wanted to break Jesus and add him to the list of traitors who had rebelled against God. Satan wanted to entice Jesus to join forces with him against God, the Father. There could be no greater prize than a son rebelling against his father.

I proceeded in line, waiting to be baptized, hoping for some kind of special experience. But all that happened was I got wet. I must say, the experience was cool and refreshing, but I expected more. I was disappointed, and I suspected my heart wasn't right. I wasn't sure what changes I needed to make so I could have the joy others talked about. As I stood on the bank watching the others being baptized, I heard someone call out my name.

I turned to see my old friend Benjamin.

Benjamin and I had grown up in Capernaum. Later, he met a girl from Cana and moved there.

Her father owned a farm, and Benjamin worked for him, raising livestock. Over the years, I had assisted them with their investments, and they had accumulated great wealth.

As we approached each other and embraced in a friendly hug, Benjamin said, "Demas, why are you dressed that way? Have you fallen on hard times? You normally dress in such elegant attire."

I explained I had been robbed and beaten. "I've suffered extensive physical injuries, including a blow to the head, causing memory loss. The experience has taught me valuable life lessons. I'm anxious to share with you what has occurred since the last time I saw you."

Benjamin invited me to join him on his trip back home. He said his youngest daughter was getting married in about six weeks, and he wanted me to come for the wedding.

I accepted, and after buying some suitable clothes, I set out with him to Cana.

Chapter Five

That evening, we set up camp just off the trail. We gathered the firewood we needed to keep us warm on the cool evening and ward off any wild animals.

As we finished our evening meal, our conversation drifted to a discussion of old times when we were growing up in Capernaum. Life was not always easy for either of us. After our chores, we spent time learning the Holy Scriptures and Jewish traditions. We also had to learn the rules and regulations added to God's Word by the religious scholars.

When Benjamin and I grew up, Capernaum was so small that the entire population seemed like extended family. And as adults, both of us shared similar views. We were both religious skeptics. We grew up faking our belief in God and had privately shared we believed the stories of God were just that—stories. We believed the rules and regulations imposed on the people were intended to keep everyone submitted to religious authority, especially the older children and the wives, who were required to submit to their husbands. Naturally, every man in Israel supported the wifely submission rule.

I longed to share my vision of the Other Side with Benjamin, but I just didn't know where to start. I didn't want to alienate an old friend, but I was truly concerned that someday Benjamin would end up on the Other Side and suffer eternal separation from God—even worse, experience the Bottomless Canyon and the unknown events the final judgment would bring.

Looking up at the sky, I finally said, "Have you ever wondered what's up there, or if men will ever reach the stars?"

Benjamin replied, "Why do you allow your mind to dwell on such foolishness? We cannot climb to the top of the highest mountain, let alone go to the stars. Something has changed you since the last time we met. You're not that same fun-loving, hard-working guy I used to know."

"A lot has happened to me lately. I've developed an interest in the things of God."

Benjamin laughed. "Since when has Demas concerned himself with children's stories? We've discussed this subject a hundred times over the years. I thought we agreed there is no God. What has happened to you? Have you been talking to God like Moses did?"

I paused. "The older I get, and the closer I come to death, the more I wonder about these issues. Don't you?"

"Yes, but then I come back to my senses. When you die, you're dead. I'm certain of that."

"It would be a miracle if someone came back to life, wouldn't it?"

"Knowledge is power. Security is in gold. That's my motto."

"But what if you had a chance to experience God—"

"I want to experience all life has to offer, even if I cross religious boundaries. Let the Temple leaders worry about their ridiculous rules and regulations. Everyone knows they don't abide by them."

"Just because some men are hypocrites doesn't mean God isn't real."

Benjamin turned a scowl on me for the first time in our friendship. "We need to get some sleep. We have a long way to go tomorrow. Good night,

Demas. And just in case God shows up, don't wake me."

"If God shows up, you will be awakened. But it won't be by me."

As I lay there, gazing into our fire, I remembered Aggravate's comment about the final judgment. I thought about the fate that awaits all those who reject God. I had to find a way to please God. I do not ever want to experience the Other Side or even see it again.

But how much did I have to do? And how could I please God? How many people must I convince to change their ways? What did I have to do to earn eternal life with God in heaven? These questions left me confused and fearful.

Sometime in the night, as my mind raced through these questions, I heard a wild beast thrashing and growling in the distance. Normally these sounds would send a chill down my back, but I had no fear. I knew I was on a mission from God, and I knew God would protect me until I was able to complete my assignment. This knowledge gave me great comfort.

I also remembered God the Father had told me Jesus would speak to me. That had not happened yet. I peacefully rolled over and went to sleep with no concerns for my safety.

The next morning, Benjamin and I woke up early, loaded the donkeys, and headed for Cana. The trip was long and hot during the daytime, but there was no complaint from me. Even with my pain, I sensed God restoring my health. My experience on the road could have left me dead, and my experience on the Other Side made me glad to be anywhere but there.

After all, here in Israel, there was hope. There is no hope on the Other Side. Here, I could look forward to my next meal, my next cool drink of refreshing water. My senses were alive. Never in my life had I noticed the wonders of my own body and spirit, let alone life and the wonders of God's creation. I promised myself I wouldn't complain about anything anymore. My heart filled with gratefulness, and I reminded myself a hundred times that day how fortunate I was to be alive. I couldn't help but think that if people could only experience the hopelessness of the Other Side, they would do whatever was necessary to avoid it.

Now was the time to concentrate on living the best life I could. I needed to look for opportunities to speak to people, to encourage them, to change the way they lived. But how could I explain what I've experienced without people thinking I was crazy?

Chapter Six

———————— ❦ ————————

S oon we arrived at the small town of Cana.
After a few days of rest and visiting with old
friends, Benjamin and I met with his father-
in-law, Nathaniel, to talk about the purchase
of land.

I discovered the seller was experiencing serious
physical and financial difficulties, so I advised
Nathaniel not to take advantage of him when he
was down and out. I made it clear that if anyone
was being taken advantage of, I would not be able
to be a part of the negotiation. My newfound ethical standards surprised the whole family.

Nathaniel agreed. He was willing to pay the
sellers a fair price for the land, in spite of the
fact the neighbor had not always been the most
honest person in their previous dealings, or the
best neighbor.

I was thankful for Benjamin's friendship and hospitality, so I told Nathaniel I would not charge him for my services.

Nathaniel knew the normal fee for a transaction of this size: a year's wages for a skilled worker. He asked me to stay as long as I wanted, even after the wedding. But I explained that I would be leaving for Capernaum two days after the wedding so I could get home and see my family.

After a couple of meetings with the seller, we completed the deal. Both parties were satisfied, and Nathanial invited the seller and his family to his daughter's wedding.

I had been so busy, I had been unable to assist in the wedding preparations. But on the evening the purchase was complete, Nathaniel and his wife prepared a wonderful celebration dinner.

During the course of the evening, the ladies were discussing the wedding guest list, and I discovered that Jesus, some of his friends, and his mother, Mary, were going to be there.

I was thrilled to get a chance to see Jesus again, just a few weeks after the baptism.

Nathaniel wanted to make this a special day for his youngest granddaughter, the baby of the family. So he offered a special thank-you to the residents of Cana for opening their homes to the wedding guests who had to travel great distances to attend.

On the special day, during the wedding ceremony, I looked for Jesus, but there were so many people in attendance, I didn't find him until the ceremony was over. When I did, he was in discussion with four other men: Andrew, his brother, Peter, Philip, and Nathaniel. These men were to become some of the chosen ones. I remembered I was not to speak to Jesus or any of his chosen ones, so I remained silent and just had to listen.

At that time, I wasn't exactly sure, but I felt my non-contact was probably meant for those traveling with him. I was especially careful not to violate any of the rules God the Father had given me, but at the same time, I attempted to be as close to Jesus as possible in order to hear every word he spoke. I listened with anticipation each time I saw him because I thought he might call my name. There were so many people around Jesus, it was easy to get close but not too close.

On the second day of the wedding celebration, there still had been no communication between Jesus and me. Something strange was happening. I was able to stand or sit very close to him without any objection from those around him. I realized Jesus presented himself as a teacher with students. He instructed the four men with each word coming from his mouth. So I listened intently, hoping to learn as they were learning.

Although Jesus had no special appearance and it seemed he was just another Jewish teacher, his words were like well-aimed arrows hitting the mark of those who heard them. He spoke with great wisdom, and everyone agreed he was the greatest teacher they had heard in their lifetime.

I knew Jesus was the Son of God, yet I was still amazed at the things he taught. As I listened to him, I kept wondering why the Son of God would come to earth as the son of a common carpenter. Why was he dressed like a pauper instead of a king? His teachings were greater than the teachings of anyone before him, including those of Solomon, yet these teachings came from a man with the appearance of a common laborer.

I also noticed that when he spoke, he was bold and never afraid of anyone around him, never fearing who might hear. It seemed he didn't care what they were thinking. In fact, it was just the opposite. He made sure everyone around him could hear exactly what he was saying. Jesus was an open book. It was almost as if he was able to speak only the truth. He didn't hold anything back. His words were straightforward, honest, and true. His teachings penetrated the hearer's mind while his eyes seemed to look deep into the heart and soul.

Everyone in his presence quickly realized that if they didn't want to hear an honest answer, they should not ask the question. Jesus never offered a warm and fuzzy answer to a question. He wanted his hearers to remember, to question, and to examine themselves.

He spoke in a humble, loving, truthful manner, and with specific purpose, like a father to his son or daughter. As I listened, I noticed Jesus was anticipating the questions the people were going to ask, almost as if he could read their minds. As time went on, I realized he knew what they were thinking and why they asked the question.

But not everybody appreciated his honesty, sincerity, and amazing knowledge. His honesty made some people uneasy, and his knowledge made some people question where he got such a wonderful education. He was raised as a carpenter's son in a small village. They were common people, like most who were attending the wedding. All this amazed those who heard him teach and speak. It was almost as though his identity had been concealed until he was ready to begin his ministry.

Late in the afternoon on the second day of the wedding celebration, I heard his mother, Mary, tell him there was no more wine.

"Why are you getting me involved?" Jesus asked her. "My time has not yet come."

Mary turned to the servers who were with her and told them, "Do whatever my son tells you to do."

Jesus told them to fill the empty wine jars with water, and so they did. They filled them to the brim.

When Jesus instructed them to take the jars out to the party, the servers were concerned that the master of the banquet would become angry when they brought water instead of wine.

But much to their surprise, after the master sampled the contents of the jar, he instructed the servers to offer the wine to his guests.

Upon hearing these comments, and having seen what had happened, I asked the server for a cup of the wine and tasted it for myself. I was amazed. In all my travels, I had never tasted such fine wine.

I wanted to scream at the top of my lungs, "Do you know what Jesus just did?" But then I remembered what Jesus had said: "It is not my time."

I realized my silence was required, so I continued to listen and take in every word, hoping for the moment when Jesus would speak my name.

Early in the evening, I excused myself to pack for my journey home to Capernaum. I decided to say my goodbyes to Nathaniel and Benjamin and their families that evening.

I waited until Jesus and the chosen ones had retired, and then I thanked everyone for their generous hospitality. Nathaniel and Benjamin asked to speak to me privately and took me out to the stable area. They thanked me for all I had done to assist them and told me they were sending me off with a few small gifts.

At first, I refused both, but Nathanael and Benjamin were insistent. They gave me food for the trip, extra clothing, two donkeys, and a small bag of gold coins.

I was overwhelmed with gratitude. I wanted to leave with exactly what I had when I came, but they wouldn't have it. So I accepted the gifts, believing God had put it on their hearts to be generous.

The next day, Benjamin was already up when I arose. "There is much more I want to share with you, Benjamin," I told him.

He laughed and said, "I hope it's not more of that God stuff. If so, it can wait."

I wished Benjamin had been more open.

We both said goodbye, and I began my journey back to Capernaum.

Just before I left and went over the hill, I looked back at Cana and wondered when I would see Jesus again. I hoped it would be soon. There was much more for me to learn. I trusted God would arrange the times and places, but for now, I had some unfinished business to attend to. I must try to see my family and explain what had happened to me.

Upon arriving at the edge of Capernaum, I spent the night just outside of town. I had a great deal of thinking to do. What should I say to my wife and children? My eight-month absence was going to be hard to explain.

Then I thought about the two men who tried to kill me. Why did they attack me? How would they respond if they saw me? Would they try to finish the job they'd started? After all, I was the only witness to their crime.

I remembered the brutal comments I had made to my wife and children the day I left home. During my vision of the Other Side, those insensitive comments ran through my mind over and over again. I was sorry for the kind of husband and father I had been. I realized I had never demonstrated real love for my family, and I struggled to understand how I could repair the damage I had inflicted on the ones I claimed to love. I wanted to make things right, but I had no idea how.

The next morning I cautiously entered the city and proceeded directly to my home. The sight of it brought tears to my eyes. I had a vision of my wife and children waving goodbye to me the day I left on my last journey. They were all smiling, or at least attempting to smile, while I, the grumpy old man, was thinking of nothing but my trip and the time I would spend with Rahab.

How could I have been so cold to my wife and children? I thought about everything my wife had done for me. I thought about the children. How much would it have meant to them if I had hugged and kissed them goodbye?

Anxiously I approached the front door, trying to think of some way to make up for lost time. I raised my hand to knock on the door, and it flew open. A large, startled man swung the door open, unaware I was about to knock.

He collected his composure. "Yes, may I help you?"

Who was this guy? "Is Goldie here?"

"She moved in with her husband's brother, Omar. I bought this house two months ago."

At first, I was angry with her for selling our home, but then I realized she probably had to. After all, I'd been gone for nearly eight months. She had no way of knowing what had happened to me. If she hadn't sold the home by now, how would she have survived?

As I approached the door of my brother's home, I rehearsed what I was going to say. I knocked and Goldie opened the door.

"Goldie ..." I said, taking in the sight of her like never before. For a man who made his living by talking, I had no idea what to say to my wife.

"I thought you were dead."

"I know, and I'm sorry—"

"You were tired of me and the children—I knew that. In the beginning, I thought you had simply abandoned us. Then I thought you were dead. Now, seeing you alive and well after all this time, I realize you did, in fact, abandon us. I don't know why I'm even talking to you. What do you want?"

This was going even worse than I'd feared. "Goldie, you won't believe what happened—"

Goldie cut me off. "You're right, Demas, I won't believe anything you say."

"Let me explain—"

"I don't want to hear it. I know about you and Rahab. I know that as a woman, I have no rights in my marriage, but my wish is for you to leave and never come back." Her voice turned even colder. "Go away and let me consider you dead."

Then she slammed the door in my face.

I stood at that door, staring at the grain of the wood, realizing the door would never open again. And who could blame her?

Sure, I had all the authority in our marriage, and I could force her to come back to me. But somehow I didn't have the heart to do that.

I decided to visit my business partner, Eli. On the way to our establishment, I could not get Goldie and her reaction out of my mind. What if she and the children ended up at the Other Side with no hope? I didn't know if my children knew anything about the things of God or even if they believed in God. Now with the reality of the Other Side and the suffering I'd witnessed, I had to find a way to reach others so they might avoid that final destiny. As far as my own family was concerned, all I could do was pray God would send somebody to them with a message of truth so they wouldn't end up on the Other Side. I wouldn't be able to reach them. I was the wrong messenger.

As I approached my former office, I remembered I had been very hard on Eli over the years and had taken advantage of him whenever I was able. I hoped he would receive me differently than Goldie had. How nice it would be if he cared enough to ask what happened to me, where I had been for such a long time. At this point, I needed to see a friendly face.

As I walked through town, many of the same businesses were still in operation with no changes in ownership. Everyone recognized me. They just stared at me or turned away. No one asked me where I had been. I hid my face in shame even though I really hadn't done anything wrong. I wanted to shout, "I didn't abandon my family!" They clearly wanted nothing to do with me, but I didn't want them to go to the Other Side. Maybe I'd never be able to win these people to God. Maybe I should talk to people who didn't know me and my past instead.

But now I had to see Eli.

With great anticipation, I opened the door of my business, knowing what I wanted to say to Eli but fearing his reaction.

Eli was involved in a conversation with a young man I didn't recognize. His old eyes looked in my direction as I opened the door. With his second glance, Eli recognized me and gasped for air. He clutched at his chest. "I thought you were dead."

My laugh sounded nervous to my own ears. "I'm as alive as you are."

Eli just kept staring at me. As I would discover later, my presence made him realize the mercenaries had lied to him when they said they had killed and buried me.

He stood there silently gazing at me, a strange look on his face. Finally, Eli said, "You've been away a long time."

"There are some things I'd like to talk to you about." I tried hard to disguise my disappointment that he wasn't at all happy to see me—just like the rest of the town.

Worse, his disgust for me showed in his eyes. "You've been gone eight months. When you didn't return, I was forced to sell your portion of the business. I gave the proceeds to Goldie. And I'm afraid I'm busy and have no time for you. I'm asking you to leave."

I couldn't believe the way Eli was responding. I could understand his anger, but his reaction just didn't make sense. "Let me explain where I've been and why it was impossible for me to return. There is so much I want to tell you." Like the Other Side.

Eli seemed a bit taller than usual when he approached me. "All the time we were partners, you never consulted me about anything. Never once did you explain any of the financial matters of our partnership, and never once did you say you were sorry for the way you talked to me and the way you treated me. After you left, I checked the books and realized you'd been taking advantage of me and stealing my portion of the profits. So why would you think I would care to hear anything about you or where you've been? This is the last time I'm going to tell you. Get out."

Everything he was saying was true. This was exactly how I would respond if Eli had been the one to take advantage of me. "I understand. But I am truly sorry, and I'm not going to make excuses. Let me simply say I was a selfish person, and I want to acknowledge my wrongdoings. I wish there was something I could do to make things right."

I left then with no intentions of returning. Eventually, I'd have to find a way to survive, but now I had no interest in returning to my former business.

I walked cautiously around the city for a while, remembering I had received only a quick glimpse of the men who had tried to kill me. I didn't want to run into them again.

At noon, I bought some fruit from a nearby merchant and found a place to recline in the shade while I ate. For an hour, I watched and waited to see if I could find someone I knew, someone who might listen to what I had learned from my vision of the Other Side. I couldn't help but wonder who would listen to a scoundrel like me.

In time, Rahab walked past. I got up and followed her discreetly to her home. I glanced around, and when I was sure no one was looking, I slipped to the bottom of her stairs. If anybody needed to hear the message I had received from God, it would be Rahab. Even though she was a prostitute, I never felt she was evil. Circumstances had driven her to her employment. There was no question her heart had been hardened in her occupation, but I believed she was looking for truth, for something to fill the emptiness we all experience when our pleasures no longer satisfy.

I crept up the stairs and then knocked.

Slowly, Rahab opened the door. "Demas, it's been a long time since I've seen you. I thought you'd left the area or found a new friend." She looked me up and down and laughed. "Why are you dressed like a common worker?"

"It's a long story. That's what brings me here. I need to talk to you. It's very important."

"If you want to talk, that's fine." She held out her hand to receive her payment for the time she was going to spend with me.

"I just want to talk. I want to tell you what happened to me while I was away. I believe it could change your whole life."

"I know, Demas. I'm looking forward to our conversation, but first, let's take care of business."

"All you have to do is listen."

Rahab gestured in a way only a woman in her position could. "Well, that's a shame. If talk is what you want, fine. But first, let's settle the issue of money."

"I promise that what I have to share with you is more valuable than money."

She lowered her hand. "You of all people know there's nothing more valuable than money. What can I buy with conversation?"

I couldn't believe this was happening.

Then she said, "Look. I feel sorry for you. But you've been around long enough to know how this works. When you spend your money with me, you're buying my time, not my friendship. When you have some money, come back, and we'll fix you up."

She closed the door.

If even the local prostitute wouldn't take time to listen to me, who would?

Chapter Seven

———————— ∽∽ ————————

I went back to my place in the shade to sit and think. I remembered the miracle in Cana, when Jesus changed the water into wine. How did he do that, anyway? Of course, as the Son of God, he had powers. This was probably just the first of many miracles Jesus would perform.

I needed to spend more time with Jesus. I had to learn more about his teachings, about life, and about the things of God. And naturally, I wanted to witness more miracles. I guess that's just human nature.

By this time, it was late in the afternoon. I realized I had to find a place to spend the night. I was running out of options when I remembered my cousin Levi, the tax collector. Although we were blood relatives and business associates, and we thought alike on a lot of issues, such as religion and politics, I had rarely talked to Levi unless I could use our relationship for business gain.

Levi was perhaps one of the most hated people in Capernaum because he worked as a tax collector for the oppressive Roman government. He lined his pockets with the gold of the people of Capernaum and travelers passing through the city. Most of the people he took advantage of were people he had previously called friends.

Even though it may not be safe to stay at his home because people were always trying to kill the tax collectors, I decided to go and see him, in hopes of finding lodging for the night. I knew it would be more comfortable than sleeping on the streets, and I was still concerned about running into the two men who tried to kill me.

When I arrived at Levi's home, his servants recognized who I was and welcomed me in. The doors were secured so no unwanted guests could gain access. His slaves were armed with swords to defend the property, and they were busy getting the home and food prepared for Levi's return for the evening meal.

Levi had been away all day, busy with his tax-collector duties. His head slave was a man named Moss. Moss offered me a cool drink and showed me where I could relax while I waited for Levi to come home.

About two hours later, Levi arrived. One of the slaves had been sent ahead to alert him that I was there. Levi was excited to hear I was there, since he rarely had visitors come to his home. We hadn't seen each other for over a year. It was rare for any of our relatives to visit him. In fact, most of them no longer spoke to him.

When Levi walked in, we greeted each other in a warm embrace. We'd grown up together in Capernaum, and over the years, both of us had benefitted from our business relationship. Levi had become an excellent referral source. He had invested his money based on my advice and had benefitted handsomely.

The sad reality was we were two lonely men who had acquired great wealth. We had experienced most of what life had to offer, and yet neither of us had any kind of lasting happiness. Our self-centeredness, our greed, and our selfishness had robbed us of the simple pleasures and joys of life. It seemed the more we had, the more we had to worry about. We worried about losing the things we had acquired and worried about what might be stolen from us. There was no lasting peace or joy, only constant stress. Both of us found it hard to sleep. I remembered those feelings very well before I lost everything. It's interesting now that the things I valued the most were gone, but so was the stress.

The hatred for Levi and other tax collectors was so great, they had to have armed guards protecting them at all times, even when they were trying to sleep. It was a miserable way of life, but profitable.

As for me, the light of truth was beginning to shine. I had no desire to return to my previous life. I knew the kind of life I lived before, and I was determined not to be involved in anything that might send me to that God-forsaken place, regardless of the cost to me.

As Levi and I began our first conversation shortly after his arrival, I brought up my new hope and insight. I realized Levi might be the only person in this town who would listen, but maybe he'd be interested in a different way of life. I wanted my cousin to be the first person to have a chance to enhance his quality of life and receive assurance of his eternal destination.

As for me, I was becoming increasingly aware that Jesus was the one who knew the answers to all of life's questions. Maybe he could fill the emptiness both Levi and I felt. We needed something that would last, something with eternal significance.

As the evening wore on, Levi and I opened our hearts and shared our extensive life disappointments. We shared many secrets, but I couldn't find the words to reveal exactly what had happened to me during my vision of the Other Side. It was amazing how many similar regrets Levi and I had. At one point, Levi confessed that his disillusionments were so great and his unhappiness so overwhelming that he had considered suicide.

I told him I had also considered suicide. Life seemed meaningless in spite of my material success. Every time the world promised happiness, all I got was temporary pleasure leading to frustration and depression. How could something that seemed so right in the beginning always lead to a bad ending?

I told Levi that I had very little money and needed a place to stay, and he invited me to stay as long as I needed to. I was grateful to have a home base.

In the evening, when we both went to bed, I was not able to sleep until very late into the night. I thought it might be the new surroundings I was sleeping in, but what really kept me awake were the questions: Where do I begin? How could I explain the effects of my experience during the vision of the Other Side? Reaching out to Levi was a beginning, but I had larger plans.

Chapter Eight

Two days later, I went to the market and saw Jesus, his mother, Mary, and his brothers. People swarmed around him, listening to his teachings. As he walked along the street, every time he stopped, a crowd formed, bringing their sick, their lame, and their blind friends and relatives.

Watching him, I saw miracle after miracle. Everyone Jesus touched was healed. I was not completely surprised, since I knew Jesus was the Son of God, yet I could not stop thinking about his appearance. I couldn't believe he was dressed in such a common manner. Regardless, his teachings and the amazing miracles were anything but common.

I continued to watch Jesus among the crowd and listened intently to his teachings. It seemed every word from his mouth was directed toward me. Everything he said seemed to come from his heart. He was a master teacher, the best I had ever heard.

Two distinct groups followed Jesus. One group was those closest to him, his inner circle. The second group did not participate in the inner circle activities but always seemed to be around, watching and listening. This group I called the outer circle. The outer circle was made up of several groups: those who were truly interested in what Jesus had to say, those who were simply curious and wanted to see the miracles, and those who opposed his teaching and were looking for an opportunity to challenge him or have him arrested.

It was easy for me to mingle and interact with the members of the outer circle because it was not an exclusive group. Anyone who wanted to move in and out of the various groups was accepted. From my position in the outer circle, I was able to hear the opinions of the various individual groups, as well as witness the amazing miracles Jesus performed. I also heard there were religious leaders within the outer circle, and they spent most of their time plotting against Jesus.

I knew exactly who Jesus was, but I kept my knowledge to myself. I wanted to appear unbiased. I absorbed as much information as I could, keeping my opinion to myself. With one ear, I listened to what the crowd was saying, and with the other, I listened to Jesus. When he was teaching, everyone was silent. I looked forward to my time in his presence, because I knew something very special would occur every single day.

I made up my mind to follow Jesus every time I was able. I tried to avoid conversations with the religious leaders. They viewed Jesus as an enemy to their religion and a threat to their control over the people. There was no doubt those who followed Jesus were considered enemies of the religious leaders.

The Roman soldiers and Roman citizens were concerned that the large crowds around Jesus would create a disturbance. They were constantly on watch, ready to keep the peace by arresting anyone who caused a disturbance.

They were also concerned that Jesus might be starting a new, radical religious citizens' group. The Romans knew the citizens were angry because of Rome's invasion and control of their country. The Roman rulers were always afraid that the people might rise up again and riot against them. But the teaching of Jesus was different from anything they had ever heard, and the more they listened, the more they realized how different he was.

I was increasingly aware of the need to suppress my feelings and opinions until I had learned more. My neutrality allowed me to circulate among all the groups and hear their opinions and comments. On several occasions, I heard the religious leaders making plans and devising schemes to trick Jesus and have him arrested. For the most part, everyone else loved Jesus. Even if they were skeptical, his love won them over.

That same day, Jesus informed everyone that he was leaving Capernaum to go to Jerusalem for Passover the next day.

I struggled to decide whether to go to Jerusalem because I knew an arrest warrant waited for me there. I had discussed the warrant with Levi before I asked to stay at his home. I wanted him to be aware that there was a potential problem. Levi assured me his friends in the Roman government would protect me as long as I stayed in Capernaum, but there were no guarantees of protection in Jerusalem.

After considering all the options, I decided I must go to Jerusalem. I sensed something important was about to happen, and I didn't want to miss it.

I joined a small group of outer-circle members and followed Jesus. I knew Jerusalem would be filled with people from all over Israel and the surrounding areas. Many would come to celebrate Passover and to pay their annual Temple tax. I believed that if I stayed in groups that surrounded Jesus, I would be safe because of the large crowds.

We arrived in Jerusalem late in the morning. Jesus and his apostles went directly to a home that had been prepared for them. There was a small grove of olive trees directly behind the residence where he was staying, and the group I was with set up camp among the trees. We shared the afternoon meal in the cool shade of the olive trees, making the hot afternoon bearable.

After a time of rest, Jesus said he was going to the Temple. He would be teaching there, and those who desired to join him were welcome. Most of the group followed Jesus to the Temple. They anticipated his teachings and wanted to watch the miracles they knew would occur.

As we approached the Temple, the strong odor and sounds of animals combined with loud human voices. The scene would have been expected in a common marketplace or stable—but at the Temple? We were all visibly shaken, including Jesus.

At first, he stopped and took in the sights and smells and sounds that had become commonplace during Passover. Then we saw men converting foreign money to an acceptable currency so foreigners could pay their Temple tax. This was not only acceptable but encouraged by the religious leaders. That way, they could refuse to accept foreign currency as payment for the Temple tax.

As for the animals, most of the travelers found it more convenient to purchase the animals in Jerusalem than to transport them during their long trips. No one, including Jesus, disputed the fact that people needed these services. However, the use of holy ground as a marketplace was definitely not acceptable. To make it worse, the religious leaders had approved these activities.

Slowly, Jesus walked to a nearby stable and whispered something to the owner. The man then handed him a whip used to herd livestock.

With everyone quietly watching him, Jesus turned and walked toward the Temple.

Other than those who were with us, no one seemed to notice Jesus entering the Temple. Then came a great commotion. Animals and humans shot out the door, running and screaming. Somebody yelled, "That man inside is crazy!"

Finally, Jesus emerged, the last one to leave the Temple, and shouted, "Out with you!"

Then he turned his attention to the moneychangers. He shoved the tables onto their sides, cracking the whip. "How dare you turn my Father's house into a market!"

One by one, the merchants fled the Temple area, driven by the whip. Money scattered everywhere, but no one stopped to pick it up, and no one was bold enough to challenge Jesus as they ran from him. It was as though they knew what they were doing was wrong. Everyone, especially the religious leaders who had endorsed these activities, clearly knew this was a gross violation of the use of holy ground.

Finally, the Jewish leaders mustered enough courage to ask, "What miraculous sign can you do to prove you have the authority to do what you've just done?"

"Destroy this Temple, and I will raise it up in three days."

The religious leaders said, "It has taken forty years to build this Temple, and you say you can build a Temple like this in three days?" They believed they were talking to a mad man. No one seemed to understand Jesus was talking about his own body.

I listened intently, longing to discuss this and many other things with Jesus, but I knew I had to wait until he spoke to me directly. I could hardly wait for that moment to occur.

Over the next few days, Jesus performed many miracles, including casting demons out of possessed people. Large crowds witnessed these events and became followers, and many joined the outer circle, following Jesus wherever he went. Momentum in Jesus' ministry was building fast. It was hard to imagine he could become so well known in such a short time.

The next evening, we all came together to share our food, and Jesus blessed the meal. The evening continued with fellowship and a brief teaching, then most of the group retired, as it had been a long, hot day, and we all needed our rest.

Before going to bed, I sat on a fallen tree near the fire just behind the house where Jesus was staying. While I was sitting quietly, looking toward the stars, I began to wonder exactly where I had been in my vision of the Other Side. Jesus must have known the exact location because the Other Side was in full view of Paradise, which was Jesus' previous home.

Perhaps God had allowed others to experience the same vision. Could there be others like me who had been given the responsibility to try to reach lost and confused people of my generation?

I longed to discuss this and many other things with Jesus, but again, I knew I had to wait until he spoke to me directly. The wait was beginning to take its toll on me, but I knew it would be worth it. Maybe tomorrow ...

Then, out of the corner of my eye, I saw a man lurking in the bushes just outside the home where Jesus was staying. Suddenly, he strode from his hiding place to the front door of the home.

As he walked into the moonlight, I noticed the man was dressed in religious attire, like a Pharisee would wear. It was too dark out to see who he was, so I too hid in the bushes to see what would happen.

After he knocked, the Pharisee spoke to someone just inside the door. Within moments, Jesus emerged, carrying a lamb like a little baby or a pet. They walked a short distance behind the home and very near to where I was crouching in the bushes. Now I could clearly see the man Jesus was talking to. It was Nicodemus, one of the leading Pharisees and the man whom many considered to be the leading scholar and teacher of God's Word in the nation of Israel.

The conversation seemed friendly, but I wondered if Nicodemus had come to complain about the incident that happened at the Temple earlier in the day.

I got down on my hands and knees and crawled closer, hoping to hear what was said. I heard Nicodemus refer to Jesus as Rabbi. He said, "We know you are a teacher from God."

From God? How could anyone know where Jesus had come from? I thought John the Baptist and I were the only ones who knew. After all, no one else had heard the Father at the baptism in the Jordan. And when God the Father said, "This is my Son, in whom I am well pleased," nobody else responded as if they had heard Him. So how would they know?

Then I realized it must be the miracles. No one had ever done the things Jesus did every day.

Nicodemus said, "No one could have performed the miracles and the miraculous signs you have done unless God were with him."

He was right, and it made sense to me. If Jesus had not come from God, how else could he perform the miracles he was performing every day?

Jesus seemed to ignore the compliments. This was not unusual. He often changed the subject when people tried to flatter him. He seemed to know why Nicodemus had come, and he kept asking Nicodemus questions. Then he said, "I tell you the truth; no one can enter the kingdom of God unless he is born again."

"How can I reenter my mother's womb?"

Then Jesus went on, "I tell you the truth; you cannot enter the Kingdom of God unless you are born of water and the Spirit. Flesh gives birth to flesh, but the Spirit gives birth to spirit."

Nicodemus had a strained look on his face, clearly trying to understand.

Then Jesus added, "Unless you are born of the Spirit, you are spiritually dead and have no understanding of the things of God."

"How can this be? Am I spiritually dead? Will the things I have been teaching lead our people to eternal life? I have great knowledge of the Laws of God, but I do not understand spiritual birth." He walked away, shaking his head.

Then Jesus called to Nicodemus. "You are the teacher of Israel, but you do not understand these things? We can sit here all night and discuss the things we know. We can talk about the things we've seen. We can talk about earthly things, but if you do not believe or understand them, how will you understand the things of God?"

Then Jesus continued, "Just as Moses lifted up a snake in the desert, so shall the Son of Man be lifted up. That way, everyone who believes in Him will have eternal life."

Nicodemus said he understood the history of Moses and what occurred in the desert, but he didn't understand how that applied to what Jesus was saying.

Then Jesus said, "For God so loved the world that he gave his one and only son, that whoever believes in him shall not perish but have eternal life. My Father did not send me to condemn the world but to save the world.

"The light has come into the world, but the people love the darkness instead of the light because their deeds are evil. Whoever lives by the truth comes to the light."

Nicodemus nodded. "Everything you say is true. Now I know for sure you are the Messiah, the Son of God, and the Promised One." A perplexed look came over Nicodemus. "What shall I do with this truth? If I tell others, they will hate me as they hate you."

"You are the primary teacher of Israel. You know what you should do. You should teach what you know is true. Remember, the truth will set you free, but only if you embrace it."

Nicodemus now faced the greatest challenge of his life. Would he stand with and follow Jesus, or would he choose to remain silent? Only time would tell.

Jesus stood watching Nicodemus walk away, then as he turned back toward the house, he stopped and again looked directly into my eyes.

I thought I was hidden from sight, but Jesus knew I was there the whole time. Strangely, once again, the look in his eyes was not a condemning look. They were filled with the same love and compassion I had seen many times before. Those eyes communicated love in a new way, a powerful yet gentle way with no condemnation or condition, only love. I wanted to look into His eyes forever.

While no words were spoken, I sensed he was saying much to me with that look, and I know he knew my thoughts. Every time I experienced his eyes upon me, it resulted in a powerful form of unspoken communication.

Jesus went back into the house, and I went back to the place I had laid my bed. His teaching to Nicodemus was also meant for me. I felt privileged to have been present at this meeting where new information had been revealed to me for the first time.

When teaching, Jesus rarely said more than he had to. Everything he said was intended to teach everyone within hearing distance. I treasured every word that came from his mouth, and

I internalized them. I wanted to embed each word in my mind and heart forever.

I wondered how I would become part of spreading the good news Jesus shared with Nicodemus, especially since I didn't completely understand what Jesus meant. Nicodemus, like many of us, was looking for truth. We both knew something was missing in our lives. Something wasn't fulfilled. I knew Jesus had the truth. I subsequently found out Jesus not only had the truth but was the Truth. There was no false information in his message or in his teaching. I was coming to realize that pleasing God does not come through abiding by rules and regulations, nor does it come from doing good. Pleasing God, I was discovering, comes from submitting to faith and his authority.

The reason the teaching of Jesus was so difficult for Nicodemus and the other religious leaders to accept was because it didn't show them how to earn their salvation. For centuries, the Jews believed that their good works would earn them a relationship with God. They believed they could please God with their works by following man-made rules. The message Jesus brought was not greeted in a friendly way by the leadership of the Jewish faith. His message was in conflict with what they had taught and what they learned over the centuries. Now this "son of a carpenter" came with a new message, a message he claimed came from God. His message would change everything about worship for the Jewish people and would threaten the religious leaders' control over the people.

All the people could see the hypocrisy of the religious leaders. They imposed impossible rules on the people. Their opposition to Jesus and the truth in his message exposed the religious leaders for the frauds they had become, and it was an indictment of the corrupt religious system they were a part of.

Once again, my mind went back to my vision of the Other Side. I was beginning to understand the "born-again" experience Jesus talked about. Who could hear his message and choose a different path than his—one that would lead to eternal life and Paradise?

Just before I went to sleep, I thought how privileged I was to be near enough to hear almost everything the Son of God was saying. I couldn't wait to see what would happen tomorrow.

For the next few days, I joined other members of the Outer Circle as we traveled with Jesus. He was constantly teaching and healing along the way. Some people understood his teachings. He was straightforward in his message, and his words pierced the hearts of many who heard him. Yet some of his teachings seemed beyond the hearers' understanding and left them confused. Some hidden meaning seemed to lie beyond their human understanding. Or, in some cases, his teachings required a level of submission many people were unwilling to accept.

People came from every nearby town and village when they found out Jesus was present or was on the way. Some came to watch or receive a healing. No illness or physical disability was beyond the healing power of Jesus. Every single one was healed.

His power was so great, many people were healed simply by touching his cloak. Everyone expressed their love for Jesus, and it was obvious he loved them as well. He never placed a condition on the people for their healing. He asked only if they believed in God and told them that through this belief, God could heal them. In some cases, there was no conversation at all. He simply touched those who desperately reached out to him. No one was ever disappointed, and neither were those who just came to see and hear. He was, without a doubt, like no one they had ever seen before.

As Jesus continued his ministry, his disapproval of the religious leaders' hypocrisy escalated. He continued to refer to their false teaching. He made it very clear that they were leading people astray and misrepresenting God's plan for his people. Eternal life with the Father required God to be first in a person's life, he said, and could not be earned.

The self-righteous religious leaders called Jesus a friend of sinners, a title he did not deny. Jesus said repeatedly that he did not come for the righteous but for the sinners. This included everyone, even the religious leaders, since no one was righteous. His desire was to see everyone repent of their sin and place their trust in God. He wanted to see their lives dramatically change. "It is not the healthy who need a doctor," he said, "but the sick."

Jesus became increasingly vocal about the arrogance, hypocritical actions, and lifestyles of the religious leaders. He also pointed out that they don't understand the Scriptures. His criticism caused an angry response. Each time Jesus discussed these issues with the people, the religious leaders became outraged and more determined to have him arrested. Some even wanted him killed. Many who heard Jesus secretly withheld their comments for fear of retaliation from the religious leaders. The boldness of both John the Baptist and now Jesus gave many of the people the courage to criticize the religious leaders.

God's word was the source of His truth, which had been revealed to Moses and other chosen prophets. The religious leaders were so busy enforcing their man-made rules, they had disregarded the obvious in God's word. If they had opened their minds to the truth, it would have become obvious who Jesus was. When Jesus came right out and said who he was and where he came from, the religious leaders became enraged.

His miracles made things even worse. The leaders were supposed to be able to do anything a simple carpenter's son could. Because they rejected Jesus' claim that he was the Son of God, they couldn't explain how he was able to do the things they could not do. This escalated their anger even more. They rejected the benefits of the healings he did because those miracles damaged their pride. Their lifestyles and control of the people were being threatened, and this sin blinded them to the truth.

One evening, while we were still in Jerusalem, I was chatting with a few newfound friends around the campfire when one man mentioned he had overheard Jesus saying he was going back to

Galilee. Since the religious leaders continued to view Jesus as a threat, their anger toward him escalated each time he taught.

Jesus' popularity was growing every day, and by now he was even more loved than John the Baptist. Jesus' disciples were now baptizing more people than John ever had, but this did not offend John. In fact, one person in the outer circle said he had heard John say, "Jesus must increase and I must decrease."

When I heard this, my memory took me back to the baptism at the Jordan, when both John and I heard God speak from above, saying, "This is my Son, in whom I am well pleased." It was obvious John knew who Jesus was. John had heard from God himself. John had committed to becoming a servant of Jesus.

As I thought about what Jesus had said to Nicodemus, I thought there must be some secret meaning behind the term "born again." But like Nicodemus, I was confused about re-entering my mother's womb. I knew there was a different meaning to what Jesus was teaching, and I was determined to understand.

The next morning, Jesus called everyone together and told us he was going to give an important teaching that day at the Temple, and then when he completed the teaching, he was going on a trip to Galilee by way of Samaria. As everyone proceeded to the Temple, I was trying to decide what to do next. I wanted to follow Jesus to Galilee, but I also needed to go back to Capernaum and see Levi. I needed to find out if he needed my assistance.

At the last minute, I decided to join the rest of the crowd and follow Jesus to the Temple. When we got there, Jesus began to teach. The crowd grew larger and larger. Some of the Pharisees came out to hear what Jesus was saying. Once again, they hoped he would say something they could use against him to discredit him.

Then I noticed one of the Pharisees pointing toward me. The Temple guard began to work his way through the crowd, in my direction.

I took advantage of the large crowd and escaped. I circled around through town and made it back to the place I had stayed the night before. The guard chased me but could not catch me. I was able to elude him by using the density of the crowd to slow him down.

I stayed in the forest until the dark of night. And then I made my escape. I headed back to Capernaum without saying goodbye to anyone. In

Capernaum, I knew I would be safe. There I would have the protection of Levi and his Roman friends.

I arrived at Capernaum at midday on the Sabbath. Levi was at home, and we met and caught up on the events of the last few days. I dominated the conversation with stories about the amazing things I had seen while I was following Jesus.

Levi sat there quietly, like a child hearing a story for the first time. He eagerly wanted to hear every detail.

"I'm confused," he said. "You said the Pharisees, Nicodemus, and the other religious leaders believe Jesus was sent from God. But if they know Jesus was sent by God, why don't they listen to him? And when they see this Jesus healing people, one after another, and casting out demons, why are they at odds with him? Are they jealous of him?"

"He has compassion for the sick, for sinners, for the lost who are searching for the truth. He's not afraid to touch the untouchables. At the same time, he's critical of the religious leaders. He calls them hypocrites, broods of vipers, and false teachers. When the people hear Jesus, they know he's right, but they're afraid to say anything. One of the reasons he's so popular with many people is because he says things they would like to say but are afraid to."

Levi paused as if in thought. "Could Jesus be the promised one, the Messiah? If so, he'll know the answers to my questions about life. Where is he now?"

"He's headed to Galilee, through Samaria."

"Why Samaria? I refuse to go there."

"Levi, if you could see and hear him, you would understand the message Jesus teaches is for everyone. It comes directly from God, and it's a message of God's love for everyone. It is a gift we must receive."

"I can't leave like you can. I have responsibilities. Maybe some other time. But I truly want to meet him. For now, I have taxes to collect and money to earn. There will be another day." He shifted in his seat. "You promised you would help me if I asked. I'm interested in some property in Nazareth. Would you go and look at it and negotiate a price with the owner for me?"

"When would you like me to leave?"

"There's no rush. We have much more to talk about. I want to hear everything you remember Jesus said, especially about being born again. I want to understand what that means."

Well, so did I. "I haven't got a clue what it means or how to do it. But I'm hoping to find out more. I'm looking forward to the day when I see Jesus again. I promise I will try to find out about being born again and what the experience means."

No sooner did the words come out of my mouth than I remembered I would be unable to speak to Jesus until he spoke to me. I would only be able to listen, not ask any questions. Listening was fine, but I longed for the day he would speak to me directly and I could ask all the questions both Levi and I discussed, questions that never seemed to leave my mind.

After a few days of rest, I set off for Nazareth to negotiate the purchase of the property Levi wanted. On the way, I remembered Jesus was born in Nazareth. During my previous travels, I had been through it many times, but I had not spent much time there. Nazareth was not a city that provided much excitement. During my business trips, I had never met Jesus or his family. I was always involved in meetings with wealthy people, not poor families like Jesus'.

This trip would be different. I wanted to know more about Jesus and his family. I wanted to know about his upbringing. It didn't make any sense for Jesus to come from his throne in heaven to live this simple existence. It was beyond my understanding. The questions just kept coming to me. Why shouldn't the Son of God come like a king? He is, after all, greater than all the kings of the earth, wiser than Solomon, and I have seen his healing power. So why this lowly existence on earth?

I had to discover the answers, so I decided to investigate Jesus and his background. My business in Nazareth took only two days. I spent the rest of the time asking questions. I was cautious not to draw attention to myself, but I discovered where Mary lived, along with some of Jesus' brothers and sisters.

During my investigation, a man asked me why I had so much interest in the family. After that I stopped asking questions.

The next day, the Sabbath, I decided to go to the Temple. Much to my surprise, Jesus was there. He had returned to visit Mary, his mother, and the rest of the family. During the Temple service, when it came his turn, Jesus stood and read from the Scriptures. He stopped and looked at the audience and said, "The Spirit of the Lord is on me. He has anointed me to preach the good news to the poor and has sent me to proclaim freedom for the prisoners and recovery of sight, to release the oppressed and to proclaim the year of the Lord's favor."

Then he rolled up the scroll. He gave it back to the attendant and sat down. All eyes in the building were on him. Then he said, "Today this Scripture has been fulfilled, and you have heard it."

All spoke well of him and were amazed at the gracious words that came from his lips.

He began teaching people in their synagogue. They were amazed. "Where did this man find this wisdom and these miraculous powers?" they asked.

But then their tone changed. "Isn't this the carpenter's son? Isn't his mother Mary, and his brothers James, Joseph, Simon, and Judas? Aren't all of these sisters with us? Where then did this man get these things?" And they took offense at him.

And then Jesus said to them, "Only in his hometown and his own house is a prophet without honor. Surely you will quote this proverb to me: 'Physician, heal thyself. Do these things here in your hometown—things we have heard you have done in Capernaum.' I tell you the truth, no prophet is accepted in his hometown. Look at the prophet Elijah. He was also rejected in his hometown."

I believed by rejecting Jesus, the people were rejecting the one who sent him and rejecting the message sent by his Father. I have no doubt others were thinking the same thing.

With that, most of the people in the synagogue left, furious. His claim of prophecy being fulfilled brought swift judgment. They took charge of Jesus and ushered him out of town to a cliff overlooking the valley below. The people were so angry they intended to throw him off the cliff, sending him to his death.

As they got closer to the edge of the cliff, I objected to those standing near me. "You can't do this. He is who he says he is. I have heard his teaching, and I have seen the miracles he performed. The blind can see and the lame can walk. Jesus was sent by God. Please stop this insanity!"

I avoided looking at Jesus as I made my comments. No one heard me except those closest to me. The crowd was screaming vulgarities at him, and my voice was not loud enough for the people nearest Jesus to hear me. I was sure this was going to be the end. There were so many people, I couldn't see how Jesus could escape.

He turned and again looked directly at me, with those same compassionate eyes. I dropped my head in submission.

Then a voice came from above that only Jesus and I heard. It was the voice of God the Father. He said, "Remember, Demas, you are not to raise a hand to defend my Son. Do you remember?"

I looked skyward and muttered, "Yes, Lord."

But what should I do? They were going to kill him!

A large man standing next to me said, "Do you want to join him?"

I said, "What do you mean?"

He said, "Hold your tongue, or you will join this blasphemer as we throw him off the cliff. Since you are so quick to defend him, maybe you'd like to join him."

I said, "No, sir. I will hold my tongue. I am sorry if I said something to offend you." Of course, I didn't mean what I was saying.

I looked back at Jesus. He was standing at the edge of the cliff as the crowd approached him. Then something distracted me—I don't know what—and I looked away for a split second.

Then someone said, "Where did he go?"

I saw Jesus standing right next to the person who asked the question.

"He disappeared," someone else said.

Everyone was looking around except me. I couldn't understand why they were confused. I could see Jesus standing there in the middle of the crowd, near the edge of the cliff, but the people seemed blinded to him.

All of a sudden, Jesus walked through the middle of the crowd, completely unnoticed. It was amazing. He walked directly toward me. As he passed me, he did not stop, nor did he say anything. He simply smiled and kept going.

I turned, watching him, and then he was gone. He had simply disappeared.

As quickly as Jesus left, so did I. I wanted to slip away from the large man and his friends and avoid any of the angry crowd. They seemed determined to throw someone off the cliff, maybe just anyone. As angry as they were, that could have turned out to be me.

I left the town and returned to Capernaum as fast as my legs would carry me.

It was obvious the people of Nazareth were not ready to hear the message God sent Jesus to deliver.

As I returned to Capernaum, I discovered Jesus was moving his ministry home base there. I would be seeing him much sooner and more frequently than I had expected. By the time of our next meeting, Jesus had become a permanent resident of the city of Capernaum. His presence would have a dramatic effect on the city and its citizens.

Back in Capernaum, the first thing I did was to go to the tax booth where Levi was working. I told him many of the events of my journey. I was so excited, I almost forgot to tell Levi about the property I went to see. After I calmed down, I took time to go over those details.

Because of the violence of the townspeople, I advised Levi not to buy. Also, this particular property did not have an adequate water supply, thereby limiting the amount of livestock it would support. We both agreed Levi should look at another parcel of land in another area far away from Nazareth.

The incident at the cliff persuaded me not to visit Nazareth any time in the near future. I told Levi to avoid it too. The people of Nazareth seemed to become agitated quite easily.

As the conversation returned to Jesus and his activities, I realized Levi was more interested in Jesus than he was in the property. In my absence, Levi's burden of loneliness seemed to have magnified. He missed our companionship and long chats. The news I brought about the things I had heard and had seen gave Levi even more hope of a better life—the kind of life Jesus talked about.

Levi longed for fulfillment in his empty and aching heart. He was lonely and despised, something both of us understood. No one loved him. Nobody wanted to be friends with a tax collector except the other tax collectors, and most of them were not very congenial. The average tax collector could not be trusted.

Levi was hesitant to share his feelings with any of them. He knew they would use that information to enhance their position with the Roman officials. Also, many of them were always looking to take over another tax collector's booth, especially if it was in a prime location. The Roman officials kept a watch out for people who were not doing their job or didn't have the right attitude about their responsibilities. For this reason, Levi found himself with virtually nobody to talk to or trust until I came along.

While I was in Nazareth, Levi decided if Jesus came anywhere near Capernaum, he was going to make every effort to go and see him. He even wanted to meet with him and ask him some of the questions that were plaguing him. He wanted to know how to get peace and joy, happiness and fulfillment—things money could not buy.

We didn't realize how quickly this might occur. Jesus was on his way to Capernaum and would arrive the next day. Thousands of people had been in Jerusalem during the Temple cleansing, and word about that had spread throughout the country.

The name of Jesus had become well known to just about everyone. He was becoming a national hero. Everyone wanted to see him, touch him, and speak to him. News of his coming to an area always spread like wildfire. As soon as Jesus announced his next destination, people would go ahead of him and announce the good news.

And now he was coming here. The crowds would be waiting when he arrived. The next day people came from all over the countryside. As the travelers arrived, they announced that Jesus was on his way. As promised, he arrived the next day. His presence filled the town with anticipation. No one wanted to miss out on seeing and hearing Jesus, including both Levi and myself.

Chapter Nine

There was one problem. The next day was a working day for Levi. If he decided to close his tax booth so he could see Jesus, the Roman government would fire him, and that would be the end of his lucrative career.

The next morning, as Levi prepared to go to work, he struggled to decide whether or not to go and see Jesus. At the last minute, he decided to go to work and hope for a way to meet him before he left Capernaum.

I hadn't told Levi that Jesus was going to use Capernaum as his new home base because I wanted the two of them to meet as soon as possible. Knowing Levi, he'd put off the meeting if he knew Jesus would be around for some time.

About noon, I came to the tax booth, and I urged Levi to join the people going to hear Jesus. He was on his way and would be teaching and healing in a home just down the street from Levi's booth. In fact, the home was visible from Levi's door.

I told Levi, "We need to hurry, because a lot of people are going to see Jesus. If you want to get inside, you need to come with me right now."

Levi was just about ready to close the door of his tax booth and join me when two Roman soldiers walked by in the direction of the home where Jesus was to speak. If he went now, the soldiers would report him for abandoning his post.

"Go ahead. If I can, I'll join you later. But see if you can get Jesus to meet with me privately."

Levi had become convinced Jesus was, at the very least, a great prophet. He also believed Jesus was a man sent from God and quite possibly he was the Promised One, the Messiah, and the Son of God.

I was struggling, as he was, to understand why wealth and power did not seem to be of interest to Jesus. I was intrigued by his stories and wisdom. But his healing power was beyond human understanding. The combination of strengths on one side and what I perceived to be weakness on the other side confused me.

Levi was also confused. He was committed to meeting him, and he had told me on more than one occasion that he wanted to know more about being born again.

I proceeded to the home where Jesus was going to teach. It was a good thing I left when I did, because shortly after my arrival, the entrance to the home was closed. I found a seat close to the front. The whole house was packed with people. Many people also stood outside, trying to hear and see what was happening. Even though they were unable to get in, they wanted to get as close to Jesus as they could.

Later, Levi told me about some excitement he'd seen. He said that after I had been in the house for about an hour, four childhood friends of ours carried another man, Reuben, toward him. Reuben had been paralyzed since he was eight years old. Levi remembered the day when Reuben and I climbed trees together. Levi was below the tree, watching the two of us climb, and he was there when Reuben fell and damaged his neck and back.

As the men approached the home, they had to go right past Levi's tax booth. Levi stopped them and told them there was no more room in the house and they would not be able to get inside.

Then he asked, "Why did you bring Reuben?"

One of the men said, "We've heard this man Jesus has been healing anyone who comes to him. We want him to heal Reuben."

Levi said, "Nobody can do that. He's been paralyzed most of his life."

"We're going to get him in, one way or another." They barged past Levi on the way to the home.

Watching from the door of his tax booth, Levi saw there was no way for them to enter the home. All the doors were blocked.

Then Levi saw the men going up the stairway to the roof. They wouldn't be able to hear from there, but he could sense they had a plan.

It appeared the men were taking the roof apart. At first, Levi thought they were creating a hole so they could see and hear what was going on. But they continued to remove more and more tiles and set them aside. And then the four men lifted Reuben and lowered him through the hole in the roof, directly into the building.

Inside, I saw what was happening. I also realized it was Reuben with the other four men.

Everyone was watching as Reuben was slowly lowered by four ropes. His friends intended to drop him directly in front of Jesus. Jesus had been teaching as usual, but he stopped and watched along with the rest of us. This effort by Reuben's friends demonstrated both great determination and great faith.

Reuben's sudden entrance presented a new challenge for Jesus. Almost everyone in the home believed it would be impossible for Reuben to be healed. Everyone in town knew him, and many had helped the family in one way or another.

The religious leaders and their devout followers watched Jesus very carefully. It was a Sabbath, and they hoped to catch Jesus in a violation of their religious rules.

As his friends gently lowered Reuben to the floor, Jesus looked upward toward the four men and saw their faith. He looked at Reuben and said, "My son, your sins are forgiven."

Hearing Jesus, some of the religious leaders looked at each other, and one said, "Who does he think he is? He is blaspheming! Only God can forgive sins."

Jesus heard what they said, and he knew what they were thinking. He looked directly at their group and said, "What did you say?"

They remained silent. They were afraid to challenge Jesus because they knew the people loved him.

Then Jesus said, "Which is easier for me to say: 'Reuben, your sins are forgiven' or 'Reuben, get up, take your mat and walk'?" Again there was no response. "So that you may know I have the authority to forgive sins on earth," Jesus said to Reuben, "I tell you, get up, take your mat, and go home."

Reuben got up.

First he looked at his hands, and then he moved them. He bent his arms. He flexed his biceps, which had been fully restored.

He lifted each leg. Then he looked at Jesus with tears in his eyes and said, "Thank you. I will go home now."

Jesus just smiled.

The people in the home were astounded. They could not believe what they had just seen. Everyone in the home realized they had seen a miracle beyond their wildest expectations, and it had happened to a person from their own town.

Then someone said, "Nothing is beyond the power of Jesus."

Jesus turned and said, "With faith, nothing is beyond the power of God."

As Reuben made his way to the door, everyone parted to allow him to leave. His friends scrambled down the stairs and were waiting for him at the front door.

They embraced each other in their amazement and joy. The tears flowed as all five men walked toward Levi.

Levi could not see what had happened inside, but he could see the results. Reuben was walking.

All of a sudden, Reuben started jumping up and down. Every muscle, every nerve of his body had been restored. He was not just partially healed, he was completely healed and restored. Reuben began to jog, and all of a sudden, he broke into a full sprint, running the rest of the way toward his home.

As he ran past, Levi tried to stop him and find out what had happened, but there was no stopping Reuben. The four men tried to catch up, but they couldn't. They were exhausted from carrying Reuben all the way from his house and then lifting him up onto the roof in the heat of the day. One by one, they jogged past Levi.

Levi stopped the last man. "What happened? How did he heal him?"

The man said, "Jesus just told him to get up, take his mat, and go home."

"That's it? Just get up and go?"

"That's it." And then the man ran off.

Levi could not believe what he had just seen and heard. His boyhood friend, paralyzed almost all his life, walking and running like a young man again as if nothing had ever happened.

Now Levi realized everything I had told him about Jesus was true. He knew Jesus was not just a prophet. After what happened to Reuben, I too was more convinced Jesus must be the Messiah—the Holy One. Later, Levi told me, "He'll know how to help me find the truth that has always eluded me."

As Levi prepared to close the tax booth, he looked up and saw a large crowd, led by Jesus, coming his way. He stopped what he was doing, wanting to speak to him but unsure what to say.

He was a tax collector, standing in front of a tax booth. Jesus probably wouldn't even speak to him. Levi knew what all the Jews thought of tax collectors, and he realized Jesus was not only a Jew but also a man sent from God—a man filled with the power of God.

All of a sudden, he felt paralyzed too. But if Jesus could heal someone like Reuben, he had unlimited power. If Jesus knew he was a tax collector, he might strike him dead or even worse—strike him with some incurable disease, like leprosy. At this point, he had not discovered the real Jesus—the compassionate Jesus on a mission to save sinners like Levi.

As Jesus approached, Levi froze, almost afraid to breathe. Maybe Jesus wouldn't notice him. But at the same time, Levi longed for the courage and strength to step in front of him and ask for mercy and forgiveness. He wanted to be cleansed of all the wrongs he had done in the past. He wanted a fresh start and a new beginning.

As he stood there trying to decide what to do, his fear overwhelmed him, so he stayed put and tried to blend into the wall of his booth.

Jesus approached and walked up to Levi. He looked directly into his eyes. Levi's heart was pounding so hard, he felt it would come right out of his chest.

Then Jesus stopped and said, "Follow me."

Without hesitation, Levi closed the door of the tax booth for the last time and followed Jesus, not caring what fate might await him.

For Levi, this was a major decision, but he knew what he was doing. By walking away from his tax booth, he gave up not only his income but also the protection of the Roman government and their army. This decision would make him vulnerable to those who hated him. Not to mention that many who followed Jesus hated tax collectors and wanted to see them dead. Levi had sold his soul to the Roman invaders.

His decision was final, with no going back. Since he had abandoned his position, the Romans would replace him the next day. The Roman government was not a forgiving or patient one, and there were almost always repercussions for those who broke ties with them.

But none of these things seemed to matter to Levi. He knew what was important. Levi was on a mission to discover truth about life, and he was willing to sacrifice all he had acquired in order to find it. When I saw Levi's commitment, I was truly blessed.

Levi saw me then. He put his arm around my shoulder, and we walked away together, following the crowd.

In another part of town, two religious leaders saw Reuben running toward them, carrying his mat. They stopped him and said, "What are you doing?"

Reuben responded, "What do you mean, what am I doing? I'm going home." He explained he had been paralyzed since he was eight years old and Jesus of Nazareth had healed him. He said, "Jesus told me to get up, pick up my mat, and go home. And that is exactly what I am doing."

The religious leaders said, "This is the Sabbath. You are not allowed to carry your mat on the

Sabbath. Carrying your mat is work, and work is not permitted on a holy day."

Reuben smiled and ran away, carrying his mat.

The religious leaders were so consumed with their rules and regulations, they were unable to share the joy of this totally restored human being. How sad.

Meanwhile, Levi and I were determined to follow Jesus, no matter where the path might lead us. Jesus had renamed Levi. His new name was Matthew. He had been accepted as part of the Inner Circle, in spite of his previous life. I, in the meantime, remained a member of the Outer Circle. Daily, we both watched every move Jesus made. I longed for the moment he would call my name. I sensed I was running out of time but knew it would happen sooner or later.

Chapter Ten

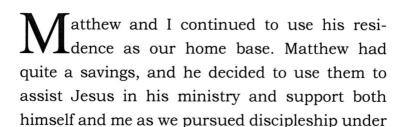

Matthew and I continued to use his residence as our home base. Matthew had quite a savings, and he decided to use them to assist Jesus in his ministry and support both himself and me as we pursued discipleship under the tutoring of Jesus.

Over the next few weeks, we witnessed increased hostility from the religious leaders, especially for what they referred to as violations of the man-made rules concerning the Sabbath. On one occasion, we were walking through a field of grain on the Sabbath. We were hungry, so we picked some of the heads of grain and rubbed them between our hands, freeing the ripened kernels to eat as a snack. The religious leaders again accused all of us of working on the Sabbath.

At first, Jesus didn't respond to the charge. He knew their hearts and waited for them to do some personal soul-searching. He hoped they would realize and come to understand their accusations were ridiculous, but they were so desperate to find a violation they could charge him with, they had become blinded to the truth. Their hearts were truly hardened against common sense.

Then Jesus said, "Have you never read what David did when his companions were hungry and in need? They entered the house of God and ate consecrated bread, which is unlawful—only for priests to eat. He gave some to his companions." He paused, waiting for a response from these who claimed to know scripture.

Still hard-hearted, the accusers remained silent.

Then he said, "The Sabbath was made for man, not man for the Sabbath. So the Son of Man is Lord, even of the Sabbath."

Jesus wanted them to understand God's purpose for the Sabbath. God the Father intended to give people this time for spiritual, mental, and physical restoration. It wasn't meant to be a time for the people to become stressed out, trying to follow complicated, man-made rules.

On another occasion, Jesus entered the synagogue on the Sabbath. There was a man present who had a grossly deformed and shriveled hand.

Jesus told him to stand up in front of everyone, then asked the crowd, "Which is lawful on the Sabbath—to do good or to do evil? To save a life or to kill?"

They remained silent, not knowing how to respond. They were afraid of being trapped and looking foolish. The religious leaders had defended and enforced laws like this for so long, they couldn't even remember who established the laws, or in some cases, how long they had been enforced.

Then Jesus said, "Stretch out your hand."

The man did, and he was completely restored.

Everyone was amazed except the religious leaders. They gathered outside the synagogue and plotted with those who would listen about how they would find a way to kill Jesus. This group of evil people somehow, through their foggy minds, perceived Jesus as a threat. But the only threat Jesus posed was his constant appeal to common sense.

The power structure they had established provided them great control over the people. No one had ever questioned their authority, and no one had ever challenged them before Jesus came. They realized if Jesus was successful in reaching the people with his message, they would lose the stranglehold that gave them power, financial resources, and control. They were concerned that people would no longer hold them in high esteem, and they would lose the privileges they believed they were entitled to as religious leaders.

They decided they must fight back and defend what they believed they were entitled to. Thus, the plot to kill Jesus began.

Shortly after the Sabbath, several of the Outer Circle members fell away. They realized the religious leaders were escalating their hostility toward Jesus, and they were afraid of the religious leaders. They believed their leaders would hold them accountable for their association with Jesus' ministry. They were concerned the price they would have to pay to follow Jesus would be too high. The wrath from the religious leaders might extend to their family members, including their children.

While some fell away, others joined. There was never a shortage of curious people. The crowds continued to grow and grow, in spite of those who fell away.

Jesus kept a close eye on all his followers, including the members of the Inner and Outer Circles. He had decided who would be the permanent members of the Inner Circle, but he had not yet told anyone who would be his closest associates.

Finally, he decided the time was right, and he called everyone together. Jesus announced the Twelve who would make up his permanent Inner Circle. He named them the Twelve Apostles. These twelve men were to be taught privately by him and then teach others. They would be sent out by themselves on occasion to spread the good news and represent Jesus wherever he sent them. In time, they would receive power from God to perform the same miracles Jesus had performed.

While I was disappointed I was not chosen, I was thrilled for my cousin Matthew, and I looked forward to hearing from him what Jesus taught in their private sessions. Most of the information Matthew would learn, he would be anxious to share with me, but on occasion, Jesus would tell the apostles not to repeat what they had been taught in secret because it was not yet the right time.

Sometimes Jesus would explain that they would understand his teachings after he had accomplished the task he had been sent to complete. On other occasions, he would mention his death and resurrection. When he talked about his death, none of us understood. Jesus would smile and say, "When the time is right, these things will be revealed to you, and then you will understand."

Still, no one wanted to talk about his death.

After choosing the Twelve, he sent them out in different directions to share with others the things they had heard him teach. After two weeks, they returned and reported the things they had experienced and learned. As they shared their experiences, successes, and failures, they gleaned wisdom and faith from each other.

On one occasion, some of the apostles were together. They attempted to cast a demon out of a child. The boy foamed at the mouth and suffered from convulsions. He rolled on the ground and sometimes into the fire. In frustration, the apostles brought the boy to Jesus.

Jesus promptly cast out the demon and restricted it from coming back to the boy. The apostles were amazed, and they asked why they were unable to cast out the demon.

Jesus said, "These things require prayer. Remember, the power comes from God the Father, not from you." He went on, "My Father is at work all around us. You should look where you see the Father working and ask him how you can join him in his activities. Your task is not to think of things to do for the Father, but to join him where he is already at work."

"How will we know?" they asked.

Jesus smiled and said, "Seek, and ye shall find. Knock, and the door will be opened. You must seek God with all your heart. God the Father must come before all things, and then he will reveal these things to you." He wanted them to understand that sensing the desires and agenda of the Father would come easier to them as their relationship grew more intimate.

And then they said, "Please teach us how to pray."

Jesus said, "Pray like this: Our Father, who art in heaven, hallowed by thy name. Thy kingdom come, thy will be done on earth as it is in heaven. Give us this day our daily bread, and forgive us our trespasses as we forgive others. Lead us not into temptation but deliver us from evil, for thine is the kingdom and the power and the glory forever and ever, amen. Do you understand?"

They all said, "Yes."

He said, "You say you understand, but do you?"

There was no response.

"Let me explain further. There is a prayer for which the Father's answer will always be 'yes.' That prayer is when you acknowledge your sin and admit you have done wrong and ask forgiveness. If you repent, God will be faithful to forgive.

If you are sincere, the Father will always forgive your sins."

Then Jesus said, "Remember even before you come to the altar before God, you must deal with your unforgiveness."

One apostle asked, "What if one person continually sins against you? Must you continue to forgive them over and over again?"

Jesus said, "How many times do you want God to forgive you?"

They responded, "Every time."

"Then do likewise. Never forget all sin is ultimately a sin against God. God is holy. Sin is not allowed in his presence. If you desire to dwell in his presence, you must learn what you must do to abide with him. These things I will teach you." Then Jesus said, "I am the truth, I am the way, and I am the life. No one comes to the Father except through me. Follow me, and I will show you the way."

No one knew the way, but we all knew Jesus knew the way, so we listened intently.

The next morning, a crowd of people waited for Jesus when he arose from his night of rest. He went out to the mountainside and began to teach, saying, "Blessed are the poor in spirit, who acknowledge their sinful nature, the spiritually bankrupt, for theirs is the Kingdom of God. Blessed are those who mourn, for they shall be comforted. Blessed are the meek, for they shall inherit the earth. Blessed are those who hunger and thirst for righteousness, for they will be filled.

"Blessed are the merciful, for they will be shown mercy. Blessed are the pure in heart, for they shall see God. Blessed are the peacemakers, for they shall be called sons of God. Blessed are those who are persecuted because of righteousness, for theirs is the Kingdom of God. Blessed are you when people insult you and persecute you and falsely say all kinds of evil against you because of me. Rejoice and be glad because great is your reward in heaven.

"For in the same way, they persecuted the prophets. They were sent with a message of truth from my Father. You are to become the salt and light of the earth, but if salt loses its saltiness, how can it be made salty again? It is no longer good for anything. You will become the light of the world. If you do these things I teach you, the light will expose the darkness in the world. Do not hide your light. Let it shine before everyone. The good things you do shall be done in the sight of the world. That way, the world will see my love through your actions. The glory for these expressions of love belongs to my Father. That way others will be drawn to the light. Everything you do, do it so others will experience the truth that has been revealed to you.

"Do not think I have come to abolish the law and the prophets. I have not come to abolish the law but to fulfill it. Anyone who breaks any of these commandments and teaches others to do the same will be called the least in the Kingdom of Heaven. But whoever practices and teaches these commandments will be called great in the Kingdom of Heaven. For I tell you unless your righteousness surpasses that of the religious leaders and teachers of the law, you will certainly not enter the Kingdom of God."

The people looked at each other. They believed Jesus had been sent by God. His teachings required high standards. They believed they had to live a life that would justify entrance into heaven by the standards Jesus had revealed. They even questioned whether the religious leaders were qualified, since they lived like hypocrites.

Jesus knew what they were thinking and added, "I tell you the truth—the man who does not enter the sheep's pen by the gate but climbs in some other way is a thief and a robber. Do you agree?"

They all said, "Yes." The people understood many claimed to be holy but for the most part, it was an exterior holiness. They did all they could to appear holy and claim to be righteous.

Jesus went on, "When a shepherd calls a sheep by name and leads him out, the sheep will follow him because it knows his voice." Then he said, "I am the Good Shepherd. The Good Shepherd will lay his life down for his sheep. I know my sheep, and my sheep know me. I know the Father and he knows me. I will lay my life down for my sheep. When this occurs, remember, no one will take my life from me. I have the authority to lay it down and take it up."

After his teaching, some of the Jewish leaders were divided. Some secretly supported his teaching, and some thought he was mad. Others were angry.

One religious leader said he called "our" Heavenly Father "my" Heavenly Father. He was identifying himself as the Son of God. "This man is not the Messiah. When the Messiah comes, he will be a king, not a carpenter. He will be the king who will conquer the world and release us from Roman bondage."

They were certain the Messiah would not be born in a stable, as Jesus had been. They also believed he would not be raised as the son of a carpenter.

At this time, a few more were convinced to leave Jesus, and they fell away. Others remembered Jesus was the one who had opened the eyes of the blind and had healed the lame and the disabled. Many had been healed themselves. Those who had been healed supported and followed him and were offended by the people who had called him common. They claimed they would never fall away. They knew he was anything but common. They believed Jesus and only Jesus provided assurance of a way to spend eternity with the Father in heaven. They also believed Jesus when he said, "I came from the Father. I know the way; follow me and I will show you the way." He was telling the truth.

On the other hand, the religious leaders were saying, "Here are the rules. Pay your Temple tax, tithe from your earnings. Our Father is a just God who will repay you for your faithfulness and your good deeds." They wanted the people to think they could earn eternal life through their efforts. This was something Jesus taught against, and every time Jesus exposed their false teaching, the religious leaders were enraged.

Several members of the Outer Circle gathered to discuss Jesus' words. One man said, "If I needed to go to Jerusalem and did not know the way, would I ask somebody from Jerusalem, or would I ask somebody who'd never been there?"

I spoke up and replied, "I agree. He is the Son of God. It's obvious he has been sent by the Father. If anyone would know the way here, he would know the way back to the place he came from. If you follow someone who's never been there, you might as well follow a blind man."

With that comment, some of the religious leaders shook their heads with disgust and walked away.

The next day, Matthew told me Jesus called the twelve apostles into a private meeting. They met and they prayed. After a time of prayer, Jesus asked the apostles, "Who do the people say I am?"

"Some say you are John the Baptist. Others say you are Elijah. And still others say you are one of the prophets who lived long ago and has come back to life."

Then Jesus said, "But what about you? Who do you say I am?"

There was silence for a moment, then Peter answered. "You are the Christ, the Son of God. You are the Messiah."

Jesus warned them not to tell anyone what Peter had said. Then he said, "The Son of Man must suffer many things and be rejected by the religious leaders. He must be killed and on the third day, he must rise to life." Then he said to them, "If anyone would choose to follow me, he must deny himself and take up his cross every day. You must understand, whoever wants to save his life will lose it, but whoever loses his life for my sake will save it. Many people will pursue the riches of this world. Even if they gain all the world has to offer, what good would it be if they lost their soul? If anyone is ashamed of me and my words, I will be ashamed of him when I come in my glory and in the glory of the Father and the holy angels. If you confess me before others, I will confess you before the Father on the Day of Judgment. I will say, 'This one knows my voice. He is one of mine.'"

Month after month, the teachings and miracles of Jesus continued. Everyone who was with him embraced his teaching, and their faith grew as they witnessed one miracle after another. They came to understand nothing was beyond the power of Jesus.

One day, the crowds became so large, Jesus and his apostles had to retreat to a boat anchored offshore. The crowds continued to grow. Most of the people were from Galilee and Judea. As evening approached, Jesus instructed the captain of the boat to set sail for the region of Gergesenes, which was on the east shore across the sea from Galilee, where he had been teaching.

Halfway across the sea, the wind came up, lightly at first, and then it turned into a gale. The swells grew so large even the sailors and the fishermen on board the boat became frightened. Fear grew into panic, and everyone on board thought they were going to die.

The other boats stayed as close together as was safe, next to the one Jesus and Matthew were in. My boat was right next to theirs. During the storm, the sound of the roaring sea was so loud, I could only give hand signals to Matthew as we tried to communicate. We both wondered if this would be the last time we would see each other.

Then the boats began to take on water, faster than we were able to bail it back into the sea, and we all started to sink. I noticed Jesus was not in sight. It seemed everyone on his boat was scurrying around, but he was absent from view.

Suddenly, he appeared. He had been sleeping. He looked across directly at me and smiled, just like other times, but this seemed an unusual time to smile.

Then, in a loud voice, Jesus said, "Why are you so fearful, you of little faith?"

It's amazing how his voice projected loud enough for everyone on all the boats around him to hear. And he said, "Silence. Be still!"

Almost as quickly as the storm had begun, it was over. Without another word, Jesus returned to his place of rest, inside the hull of the boat.

For a few minutes, no one said a word. We were all in shock. We couldn't believe what we had just seen. This roaring storm simply subsided at his command.

Matthew finally broke the silence, and he called across to me. "What kind of man is this? Even the winds and the sea listen to him and obey!"

I responded, "He is who he says he is. After this, no one should question him. He has come with the authority of God." Once more, Jesus had demonstrated his authority over God's creation.

The next morning, we anchored our boats. We were greeted by two demon-possessed men who had come out of their place of hiding in a graveyard near town. They were filthy dirty. Their clothing was in shreds. They were fierce in appearance as they charged down the hill toward the boats.

Jesus went out to meet them, completely unafraid. The rest of us stayed in our boats, hiding for our security.

As the men approached Jesus, they suddenly stopped. It appeared they recognized him. They dropped their heads and fell to their knees in submission, not looking into his eyes.

Suddenly, the demons possessing these poor souls began to speak at once in a panicked voice. "Why are you here, and what do you plan to do with us?"

Jesus did not respond, nor did he show any fear.

The demons began to beg. They said, "Jesus, you are the Son of God. Have you come here to torment us?"

He said, "What is your name?"

They said, with multiple voices, "Legion, because we are many." Then they said, "Do not cast us out to wander. Please allow us to go into the herd of pigs."

The herd was nearby, and Jesus granted permission as he simply said, "Leave." As the demons left, both of the men were cleansed immediately.

When the demons entered the herd, the pigs instantly began to run in circles. They were highly agitated and some rolled around on the ground. Then they gathered in a group, snorting and sneering and frothing at the mouth, a strange, glazed-over look in their eyes.

Then, almost as if someone sounded a trumpet with a signal to charge, the whole herd of pigs began to stampede. They ran up and over a slight knoll, then down a steep embankment leading directly into the sea. Not one of the pigs survived. They were all drowned.

Several of the townspeople, including two Pharisees who were watching, approached Jesus and the two men who had been cleansed of the demons. Everyone was amazed at what had just occurred. Some of the relatives of the two men were crying and embracing them. They had not been able to get near them since they had been possessed by the demons. After the reunion of their family members, the two men approached Jesus to express their gratitude, and they asked if they could join him in his ministry. They said, "We do not care where your ministry leads us. We promise to follow and serve you diligently."

Jesus said, "No. Go home and enjoy your families, and tell everyone about the miracle God performed here today."

Then the crowd brought Jesus another demon-possessed man who was both deaf and blind. And Jesus healed him also.

The Pharisees were fuming with jealousy when they saw how the people responded to Jesus. But there was one person in the crowd, other than the Pharisees, who was not very happy with Jesus. The owner of the herd of pigs was a wealthy man who had a great deal of influence with the people in the town. Some of his friends approached him and said, "This man Jesus has caused you great financial harm. You have lost your entire herd. Are you angry?"

Everything had happened so fast, the man had not considered his financial losses until it was brought to his attention. The two Pharisees and the owner of the pigs raised their voices and accused Jesus of doing miracles in the power of Satan. Other owners of livestock began to join them in their concern that Jesus might cast other demons into their herds.

Jesus already knew what they were thinking, so he responded. "Every kingdom divided against itself will be ruined, and every city or household divided against itself will not stand. If Satan drives out Satan, he is divided against himself. How can his kingdom stand?" Then he turned to the two Pharisees and asked, "If I drive out demons by Satan, by whom do your people drive them out?" There was no response. "But if I drive out demons by the Spirit of God, then the Kingdom of God has come upon you. He who is not with me is against me, and he who does not gather with me scatters. And so I tell you, anyone who speaks a word against the Son of Man will be forgiven, but anyone who speaks against the Holy Spirit will not be forgiven, in this age or the one to come.

"You are a brood of vipers. How can you, who are evil, say anything good? The things coming from your mouth come from your heart. The good person says good things about the good stored up in them, and the evil person brings evil things out of the evil stored up in them. But I tell you all people will give an account on the Day of Judgment for every careless word they have spoken. For by your words, you will be acquitted, and by your words, you will be condemned."

Then they said, "Show us more miracles."

Jesus responded, "The wicked and adulterous generation asks for miraculous signs. But no more will be given except the sign of the prophet Jonah. For as Jonah was three days and three nights in the belly of the huge fish, so shall the Son of Man be three days and nights in the heart of the earth."

The townspeople were careful in choosing their words before speaking to Jesus. They were also concerned more demons might be discovered, and those demons might be cast into other herds of livestock. They didn't want to suffer any additional financial loss, so they expressed their gratitude for the return of their two friends, but they asked Jesus to move on to another city and not spend the night with them. Jesus understood their concern and was not offended. He moved on, knowing he had completed his work in this town.

Those who witnessed the accounts of that day realized the hostility toward Jesus had escalated to a new level, both spiritually and physically. Jesus had demonstrated God's power over Satan and his demons. In spite of the large number of demons, they were no match for Jesus. They had no authority over him, and they were required to respond to his commands promptly. The demons were not used to being submissive to anyone. No one had challenged their authority until the arrival of Jesus. For many centuries, they enjoyed uninterrupted freedom to harass the people of earth and to lead the spiritually confused astray— including the religious leaders. Only when God himself intervened and set them in their place were they required to submit.

It didn't take long for news to spread throughout the entire spiritual world. Satan recognized his forces had become demoralized. Jesus was one step ahead of them everywhere he went. He used love to overcome hate. He used joy to overcome sorrow. He used peace to overcome fear. His plan was perfect and it was successful for anyone who put their faith in Him. Hearts were being changed, and everywhere Satan looked, he was losing ground. Satan's stranglehold on mankind was being shaken to its core by Jesus, and Satan was enraged.

In the past, Satan had become very successful by appealing to the human heart's weakness. His most effective methods included appealing to humans through sexuality, pride, arrogance, anger, unforgiveness, the lack of self-control, and self-reliance. It had been easy to lure humans away from God's plan because Satan knew humans had been given freewill, and he knew humans have a sin nature. Even the religious leaders had become pawns in Satan's hands. Their appetite for power over the people, combined with their arrogance, made them anxious and willing participants in leading the people away from the plans God had made for them. The leaders developed their own plans, thinking they were superior to God's plan, though they would never admit it.

After his baptism, Jesus had spent forty days and forty nights in the desert, fasting and praying.

Then the devil's temptations came. Although he was God's son, he was still in human flesh, and his flesh was pressed to the limit through the desert experience. After multiple attempts to have Jesus submit to him, Satan realized Jesus would be his greatest challenge. This was a challenge Satan thought he could win but one in which he would never experience victory. Satan had underestimated Jesus but quickly found that while Jesus was in human flesh, he had not given up his relationship with the Father.

Although Jesus had the power of the Creator God, he was still committed to doing the Father's will. He made it clear he did nothing on his own. Jesus was constantly looking for the opportunity to join his Father where his Father was already at work. His power came to him through submission to the Father, not through forceful actions, but by being a servant. This was the example he set for everyone who followed him.

Satan thought in order for his kingdom to survive, Jesus had to be destroyed. He set in motion the first phase of his plan by encouraging anger and jealousy among the religious leaders. Then he attempted to break down the apostles. He believed if he could cause them to doubt, he could prevent the spread of the truth Jesus was teaching.

Before leaving the area, Jesus called the members of the Inner Circle and the Outer Circle together and gave them an important update regarding the spiritual battle. He said, "The Light has come into the world, and the darkness has been trying to hide or disguise itself as the Light. But the truth will expose the darkness. Then the darkness will become angry because it has been exposed. But the light and truth will prevail. Remember, nothing will be left unexposed. The evil one will come against you, but do not be afraid. He will not be able to harm those who have placed their faith in God. The battle belongs to the Lord, and he will prevail. When Satan comes against you with his temptations, flee from them. Do not trust in yourself. Put your trust in God alone. God is the one who holds your future and the future of the world in his hands. He loves you and will defend you. Even if you lose your life here on earth for my sake, you will save it for eternity. Fear the one who holds your eternal destiny in his hands, not the one who wants to steal your eternal reward.

"Remember Adam and Eve. Consider their loss. Adam and Eve forfeited their right to live in the Garden of Eden because they did not flee Satan. Learn from their experience because your response to his devious methods can lead to eternal consequences. Again I tell you, I am the way, the truth, and the life. Follow me. I will show you the life the Father has planned for you. You will experience joy and peace and happiness. Not as the world can provide, but as the Heavenly Father provides.

"Do not settle for a cheap substitute. Accept only the best from the one who loves you. Never forget the evil one is deceptive and cunning. He is your enemy. He may appear to be your friend when he offers his temptations, but his goal is to destroy you, discredit you, and grieve our Heavenly Father. You were created in God's image, to enjoy fellowship with the Father and myself. You were created to bring glory and honor to God. Do not grieve God by your actions. Bring him the gift that has eternal value. Love God with all your heart, and if you love God, obey his commandments. Do these things as an expression of love for your Heavenly Father. Lastly, remember when you receive or plant good and bad seeds, you will reap what is sown. The farmer knows you will always reap what you sow, more than you sow, and later than you sow."

After the teaching, they retreated to the mountains nearby and spent the night. The next day, Jesus sent the chosen Twelve from the Inner Circle in pairs to six locations. I wanted to stay close to

Jesus, just in case he might call my name, but at the last moment, I followed Matthew and another apostle. I watched from a distance, sensing I should not join them.

The apostles took the teachings Jesus had given them and the authority to cast out demons. They were also given the authority to heal the sick and the lame.

I was amazed as I watched Matthew, happy to see how God was using him. I kept thinking how just a short time ago, Matthew was sitting in his tax booth, taking advantage of everyone he could, but today, he was being used by God Almighty in his work here on earth. What an amazing miracle God performed in Matthew's life. If he could use Matthew, he could use anyone, even me. I realized the things I previously thought important were no longer the driving force in my life. I was changing, and it felt good.

Matthew's conversion was evidence that God could do what he wanted with any person who had truly repented from the life they had been living and had asked forgiveness for their sin after surrendering their life to God's authority and service. Matthew had truly become a new person, and it had happened in such a short time. It was as though the person he was before no longer existed.

Perhaps this was what Jesus meant by being born again—born into a new life. Whatever was happening, I could see it was good for both Matthew and me. The joy was written all over our faces.

I remembered what Jesus had told Nicodemus about being born again. I also wanted to go through the born-again experience. I wanted to be completely changed, like Matthew, but I didn't know how. One thing was certain: I still had the responsibility to tell others about the need to change their lifestyle or suffer the consequences. Maybe that would earn me the right to have God change me.

The problem was, every time I tried to talk to someone, they were too busy. They weren't interested, or they didn't want to discuss religion. I became increasingly frustrated, and I was concerned God would run out of patience with me and my failures. If things didn't change soon, God may take me to the Other Side and leave me there. That was the last place I wanted to go. I had seen all I wanted to see in the vision God had given me.

I longed for a close relationship with Jesus, similar to the experience of the members of the Inner Circle. Maybe if I could be successful in my efforts, God would reward me. So I decided to press on, doing my best with the tools God had provided for me. I promised God and myself that I would use every opportunity he gave me and would talk to everyone who would listen. I was becoming increasingly bolder with every attempt. Sooner or later, somebody would listen to me. I had to keep trying.

In the meantime, the apostles were experiencing amazing results. People were listening and lives were being changed. The people believed and many were healed. Those who were demon-possessed were freed from their bondage.

News continued to travel all across Israel, and it also traveled across the spiritual world. Satan, the self-proclaimed king of the Other Side, was fuming. During the preceding four hundred years before the birth of Christ, no one had received any communication from God, as He had withdrawn His prophets. Many of the people had rebelled against Him and were worshiping false gods. As a result of mankind's rebellion, Satan had experienced unlimited access and influence on all the people of the world. He took this opportunity to exploit and corrupt humanity.

The corruption of mankind is a simple task because of the sinful nature. The religious leaders attempted to reestablish a way for the people to worship and have fellowship with God, but they did it through burdensome rules and regulations that even the religious leaders couldn't keep. They looked good on the outside, but their hearts were filled with corruption. Jesus referred to them as whitewashed tombs, clean on the outside but corrupt and dead on the inside.

Satan knew their weakness and took advantage of them. It was easy since he knew their greedy hearts and their thirst for power. Using the religious leaders required little effort on Satan's part, as they were like clay in the hands of a potter who created useless, grotesque objects.

That was then, but now Satan's army was becoming demoralized. Jesus had demonstrated his authority over his creation, and now he was demonstrating his power over Satan's troops. The apostles had been given the authority over Satan's troops as well.

As the crowds continued to follow Jesus and accept his teaching, Satan became increasingly concerned about how many more converts would join the Jesus movement. Satan also was concerned that the new converts might be given the same authority. He couldn't wait any longer, so he decided to launch a master plan in an attempt to destroy Jesus and his ministry.

He knew he could not outsmart or overpower Jesus. He had already tried that during the time of temptation in the desert. He decided a frontal attack would be a waste of time. So he gathered his troops and split them into four groups. Each group consisted of his most loyal and trusted servants. They were assigned to complete four different tasks.

The first task was easy because the effort had already begun: turn the religious leaders against Jesus. Some of the leaders recognized that Jesus had been sent by God. How else could he perform miracles? But they were a small minority. It took little effort to convince the group in the middle that Jesus was a threat to their established religious order, of which they saw themselves the holy caretakers.

Once the demons had the religious leaders riled up and under their control, the next step was to convince them to kill Jesus. Once again, it took little effort to convince them. The leaders saw Jesus as an enemy of everything they believed in and of their lifestyle. Before long, meetings were taking place all across Israel. The main topic was how to trick Jesus into committing sin that would require the death penalty. The greatest human minds in Israel were working on these plans.

The second group was sent to the home of Herod the Tetrarch and his lover, Herodias. John the Baptist was being held in prison by Herod. But he had not harmed him because Herod knew the people loved John. He was afraid that if he harmed John, the people would be outraged and possibly riot, so he simply held him in prison.

Satan knew Jesus loved John. They were cousins, and John had become a follower of Jesus. Satan wanted to hurt Jesus any way he could, so he set in place a plan to have John destroyed. Satan believed the death of John would affect Jesus in a negative way, and he also believed this would slow Jesus down in the progress of his ministry.

John had been very critical of the relationship between Herod and Herodias, the wife of Herod's brother Philip. On more than one occasion, John called their relationship an act of sin against God and Herod's brother. He said Herod and Herodias would be judged for their adulterous relationship. Herod knew this was true, so he and Herodias were careful, but their passions for each other clouded their judgment. Both wanted John to be permanently silenced, but the question was how they could accomplish that without outraging the people.

Satan's plan was set in place and began on the evening of Herod's birthday party. Herod's niece, Salome, the daughter of Herodias, was called on to perform a highly seductive dance for her uncle and the guests who attended the party.

Herod was so enthralled with his niece's performance that when she finished dancing, he called her over and told her she could have anything she desired, up to half of his kingdom.

Salome ran to her mother and asked what she should ask for. Herodias was fuming with jealousy, watching Herod leering at her daughter. Herod's attraction to Salome was nothing new. Satan and his demons were aware of it, and they constantly whispered thoughts of perversion into Herod's mind.

When Herodias finally stopped fuming and came to her senses, she remembered her daughter's question. Herodias saw an opportunity to get even with John for exposing her sin. She realized this was her chance to get rid of John, once and for all.

She told Salome, "Ask for the head of John the Baptist on a platter."

Herod had made a thoughtless vow to Salome, and he was obligated to fulfill it. He gave the order, and the head of John the Baptist was delivered to Salome the same night.

Herod was extremely sorry for both the promise he had made and the order that followed. He knew Herodias was behind the request from Salome, but he did not hold it against her. He was the weak one in the relationship, unable to control his passion and physical desires.

When Jesus received the word about John, he was visibly shaken. He called his followers together and told them what had happened. Then he said, "If anyone would come after me, they must deny themselves and take up their cross and follow me. For whoever wants to save their life will lose it, but whoever loses their life for me and the Gospel will save it. What good is it for a person to gain the entire world and lose their soul?"

Then he asked, "What can a person give in exchange for their soul? If anyone is ashamed of me and my words, I will be ashamed of them when they come before the throne of my Father on the final judgment day. In that day, many will come to me and say, 'Lord, we did mighty things in your name,' and I will say, 'Go away from me. I never knew you.'"

Then Jesus went away and prayed by himself.

The third group of demons was sent by Satan to observe the activities of both the Inner and Outer Circles. Satan had instructed them to be especially attentive to conversations involving the chosen Twelve, looking for character weaknesses of those closest to Jesus. They were to watch for anyone with a flaw—someone they might use to betray Jesus.

Jesus knew of their presence and tolerated it because it had already been determined who his betrayer would be. Jesus also knew exactly when and how the betrayal would take place.

It didn't take long before Satan knew who the weak one was and proceeded to plant evil thoughts in his mind. The betrayer didn't need much encouragement because he had already decided what to do. He was dissatisfied with the passive approach Jesus used with the Roman government, and he was especially opposed to paying taxes to the oppressive Roman invaders.

Nevertheless, Satan and his demons began daily assaults on the weak one. It was only a matter of time until they would wear him down, and he would completely yield to the temptations. At that point, he would commit to what he thought was his plan of deceit, leading to the arrest of Jesus. Once he was committed, there was no turning back.

The fourth group was assigned to agitate the crowds that followed Jesus. Their job was difficult because the people loved Jesus, and Jesus loved those who followed him. The average follower was a person looking for answers to life's questions. People were searching for the truth and hoping for a better way of life.

The demons assigned to the followers tried to determine who the skeptics were and who the true believers were. Their job would take the longest to accomplish, but they were tenacious in their efforts to cause doubt and division. They had received instructions not to return until they'd completed their assignment. These demons were relentless at their task. They were even able to influence the dreams of the people they chose to harass.

I thought long and hard about Jesus' teachings on losing your life and how to keep it. I wasn't sure at this time what my response would be if I was called upon to surrender my life for the cause of Jesus. My desire was to reach a level of commitment where I would be willing to give up everything, including my life here on earth, if necessary. By now, I had come to love Jesus and everything he was teaching.

I was also certain I would do anything to avoid returning to the Other Side.

A short time later, Jesus rejoined the apostles, who were sharing about their travels. Everyone was excited and amazed at what God had used them to accomplish. Their faith had grown immensely as they saw firsthand what God could do through them.

Jesus reminded them that the things they had seen and accomplished were not because of them or their efforts. These things were the work of God, and he alone was to receive the praise and glory.

Jesus used the example of Moses and King Saul to show them how serious the penalty would be if they took credit for something God had done. He said, "Disobedience kept Moses out of the Promised Land, and it cost King Saul his throne. God's plan is to use you to demonstrate his power and love for his creation. As you give credit to God for the things he has done, others will be drawn to him. As they acknowledge their sin, ask for forgiveness, and put their faith in God, they too will receive the gift of eternal life. Now follow me, and I will make you fishers of men."

One day Jesus asked everyone to sit down. He began to teach them about the things of God. He saw they were hungry for truth and were looking for the meaning of life. They wanted to know why they felt unfulfilled, regardless of their personal accomplishments. Many had complained that when the day was done, they had nothing to look forward to except going through the motions of the next day. They had no joy or fulfillment.

Jesus knew their thoughts and explained that they were created to experience an intimate relationship with God the Father, but sin had broken the relationship and made it impossible for people to experience the love and intimacy of God. However, God wanted to shower his affection on his creation. Jesus said, "If you've seen me, you've seen the Father. The Father and I are one. If you follow me and make my teachings part of your daily life, I will show you how to experience true joy, peace, happiness—the things God always intended for you. Follow me, and you will experience fulfillment. Follow me, and your life will never be boring again."

As he continued to teach throughout the day, the crowds grew. People came from every region. Toward the afternoon, the apostles came to Jesus and told him they thought he should stop teaching and healing so everyone could go to the nearby towns and get something to eat, as they had not eaten all day.

By this time, the crowd exceeded five thousand men plus women and children. Jesus turned to the apostles and said, "You give them something to eat."

They looked at each other in wonderment and asked, "What is he saying?" One of the Twelve said, "We have no money. Even if we did, where would we find enough food to feed everyone?"

As they stood there, pondering his instructions, Jesus spoke again. He said, "How much food do we have?"

All they could find were five loaves of bread and two fish that a young boy had brought for his lunch. Jesus asked everyone to sit down. Then he took the bread and the fish, looked up to heaven, and gave thanks for what God had provided. Then he began to break the bread and the fish into pieces.

As Jesus prepared the meal, I walked around the perimeter of the crowd. I repeated the same message I had heard Jesus share many times before. I had memorized his teachings, just as many in the Inner Circle had done. Now I repeated the same words again and again as I walked around the crowd. "Repent; the Kingdom of God is here." Then I added, "This is Jesus. Jesus is the Son of God. No one comes to the Father except through him. Listen to him. He holds the keys to eternal life with our Heavenly Father. You must have faith in him and his teachings."

As I walked around the crowd, repeating my plea, some of the people ignored me, while others looked at me as if I had lost my mind. It was as if they could not hear what I was saying, or they acted as if I didn't exist. Not one single person engaged me in conversation or responded to my pleas. I looked for someone, anyone, but no one provided an opportunity to share the things I had learned.

There was something missing in my message. It seemed I had the right words, and I knew the audience was looking for answers, but when I spoke the same words Jesus spoke, I got no response.

When I spoke, I did not have the same power as Jesus had. I came to know that power was the anointing of God. I had the knowledge, and it made sense for the people to listen, but the message was coming from my mouth and not my heart. Common sense is rarely a motivator for change in the human heart. If it were, everyone would have been a follower of Jesus.

After Jesus had finished preparing the food for the afternoon meal, he instructed the apostles and some of the Outer Circle members to distribute the food, beginning with those closest to him and working their way out to those farthest away.

After the meal was complete, Jesus instructed the servers to pick up any leftover food. After everyone had eaten their fill, the servers picked up twelve baskets of leftovers.

I looked in amazement, but it seemed no one else understood what Jesus had done with five small loaves of bread and two small fish. I didn't say anything to anyone about this. It looked as if Jesus did not want the people to understand what had just happened. No one asked any questions. Maybe they just wanted their hunger satisfied. They didn't seem to care where the food came from.

As the afternoon turned into early evening, the apostles came to Jesus and again asked him to send the crowd home. The people did not want to leave because they were enjoying his teaching, and they hoped to receive another free meal.

Jesus instructed the apostles to board a nearby boat and go across the sea. He told them he would catch up with them later.

The apostles went toward the boat, and Jesus proceeded in the opposite direction, up the side of a mountain, to be alone.

I didn't know what to do, as I had no boat, and Jesus seemed to want to be by himself. So I decided to stay exactly where I was and wait to see what would happen when Jesus came back down the mountain. I waited under a nearby tree.

Several hours went by, so I decided to set up camp and spend the night. Then I saw a figure in the moonlight, coming toward me. As the man approached, I realized it was Jesus. He walked just past me, toward the water, without acknowledging my presence.

I followed him, and when he reached the shore, I realized there was no boat. But he said he was going to meet the rest of the group on the other side of the sea. He stood looking out at the water for a moment then turned and again looked right at me and smiled the same smile I had seen many times before. Without a word, he turned back toward the sea, and he walked out on the water. Not in the water, but on the top of the water as if it were solid land.

I couldn't believe what I was seeing, and I couldn't take my eyes off him. His body remained straight and tall, unaffected by the movement of the water. It was as if he was gliding across the top of the water. I watched him until he vanished in the dark of night.

Once again, Jesus demonstrated his authority over the elements of His creation, this time by defying gravity. I could not wait until I caught up with Matthew, who was on the boat with the other apostles.

I pondered the events of the day: first the feeding of the five thousand men and their families, and now Jesus walking on water. And Jesus had allowed me to witness both events. I couldn't help but think what a great time this was to be alive. It was a great day, but still there'd been no verbal communication between the two of us— only eye contact.

Something happened to all who were present that day, especially me. I started this journey as an arrogant rich man and then became a broken person as I began to understand the truth about life as Jesus taught all of us. I sensed something was happening, something was changing inside me. This was the day I was to change in ways that would prevent me from ever going back to my old way of life. And that was a good thing.

As I prepared to try to get a few hours of sleep, I suddenly felt all alone. Jesus, the apostles, and the crowds were gone. What should I do next? I wasn't sure where Jesus and the apostles were going because I wasn't present when they discussed their next stop. There were no boats available late at night, and even if they were, which way would I go?

Chapter Eleven

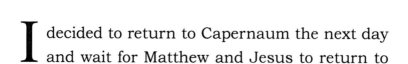

I decided to return to Capernaum the next day and wait for Matthew and Jesus to return to the home base.

Matthew told me later what had happened that evening. Jesus was walking on water across the sea. As he approached the boat, he found all the apostles on deck. Because of the direction of the wind, the boat was almost at a standstill. It was barely making progress.

As Jesus walked closer, the apostles saw him and hid themselves in terror. They weren't sure what they were seeing. They thought it might be a ghost.

Jesus called out to them. "Don't be afraid. It's me, Jesus."

Peter responded immediately. "Lord, if it's you, tell me to come out on the water."

Jesus said, "Come."

So Peter climbed over the side of the boat. The next thing they knew, he was walking on the water toward Jesus, looking directly into his eyes. The waves began to splash against Peter's legs, and he looked down at his feet. As soon as he took his eyes off Jesus, he became afraid and began to sink into the water. He cried out, "Lord, save me!"

Immediately Jesus reached out his hand and caught him. "Oh, you of little faith. Why did you doubt?"

As quickly as he climbed into the boat, Jesus looked at the sails. He realized the wind was blowing in the wrong direction. Suddenly the wind changed direction and caught the sails, and they proceeded on their journey. No one seemed to notice that the presence of Jesus brought about a change in the direction of the wind. No command was required. A simple thought on his part resulted in the wind direction change.

Jesus called all the apostles together for a lesson. He said, "Life will deliver many challenges for you to face. I have told you that you must always be in prayer to the Father and seek his advice and direction. A principle you must apply when you are praying is this: When a challenge confronts you, glance at it and then gaze at God. That is the key to overcoming the obstacles of life.

But if you glance at God and gaze at your problem, you will look inside yourself, and you will see the challenge is greater than you.

"Nothing is greater than God. He knows your struggles, and he knows your fears. Put your trust in the one who is able, and reject your desire to be in control. I tell you the truth: you must understand there are two kinds of truth. There is a truth offered by the world, and it is temporal. The truth God offers is eternal. The truth the world offers is conditional. The truth God offers is unconditional. The truth the world has to offer is ever changing. The truth God has to offer is unchanging. The truth of the world is obscure, but the truth of God is absolute. The truth of the world will deliver emptiness, but the truth of God is fulfilling.

"What kind of truth do you desire? I am the truth. Follow me and the truth will set you free. You may find my words too hard, and you may reject my words, and you may reject me. But if you reject me, you reject the one who sent me, and you reject the message he instructed me to deliver."

The next morning, they landed in Gennesaret. The people of the town recognized Jesus right away, and they sent word throughout the surrounding countryside. Before long, all the people came to hear his teaching and brought their sick and lame to be healed.

Later that evening, the apostles were quietly discussing the events of the previous night. They asked Peter how it felt to walk on water, but Peter was focused on his failings that occurred when he took his eyes off Jesus and sank. He refused to participate in the conversation and instead walked away to be by himself.

Later, Peter came back and said, "I learned an important lesson from my experience last night. The moment I took my eyes off Jesus, fear conquered me, and I sank. I know we will all face challenges in life, and they will seem impossible for us to face and overcome. But as for me, I will never again go into a challenge without focusing my eyes on the Heavenly Father. He is the one who will supply what I need. When I realized I had walked on water, I knew all things are possible with God on your side."

All the apostles agreed except one, who was already beginning to fall away. He remained silent.

Jesus, knowing their thoughts and conversation, stopped what he was doing and called everyone together again. He looked at the apostles and repeated an earlier teaching. "Many come to me and say they believe in God and believe God can heal them. Many of them are sincere. I know their hearts. But many come to me and say, 'I believe,' but they don't. They say what they think I want to hear.

"What must my Father do through me to convince those who still doubt? The blind see, the lame walk, the lepers are cleansed. The demons are cast out so people can resume a normal life. Never take your eyes off God. Never look at your inadequacies. Concentrate on the power of God, and you will see him demonstrate his power right before your eyes. I tell you the truth: if you have the faith as small as a mustard seed, you can say to the mountain, 'Move from here to there,' and it will move. Nothing is impossible for you as long as your request is consistent with the will of God."

He looked at Peter as if he knew Peter had learned the truth.

About a week later, word came that Jesus was teaching on the other side of the Sea of Galilee. I hired a boat to try to catch up with him and the others. I discovered Jesus teaching and healing in a small town on the shore of Galilee.

Just as I came up, Jesus was saying, "Soon I will go to Jerusalem, and I will suffer many things at the hands of the religious leaders and the teachers of the Law. They will kill me, and on the third day, I will rise again."

With a strange expression, Peter said, "Never, Lord."

Their conversation was personal at first, and as he said it again, it was loud enough for everyone to hear. "Never, Lord! Never should these things happen to you."

Jesus promptly responded in a loud voice, "Get behind me, Satan! You are a stumbling block to me. You do not understand the things of God, nor do you know his plans. You have spent enough time with me to know God's plan is not always understood. It's time to be silent and open your mind and your heart so you can begin to understand God's plan."

Everyone heard these words, but they were still confused. No one wanted to see Jesus harmed. They didn't understand why he was so firm with Peter. Their focus was on present events. They were blind to the plan God had put in place. It would provide the opportunity for salvation for those who put trust in Jesus and his redeeming work through his death on the cross.

Then Jesus changed the subject. "In my Father's house, there are many mansions. When

I go away, I will prepare a place for you, so when the day comes, you will be there also."

Six days later, I noticed Jesus talking to Peter again. But this time, James and John were with him. This was not unusual, as the three seemed to spend more time with Jesus than the other apostles. It appeared they were going to leave camp and take a walk.

Matthew was nowhere to be found, so I decided to follow Jesus and the others. I was careful to stay back far enough that they wouldn't notice me. I don't know why, but I sensed something was going to happen, and I didn't want to miss out.

Jesus and the apostles proceeded high up the side of a steep, rocky trail leading up the side of a mountain. This was not a normal half-hour stroll from camp. It took several hours to reach the point where Jesus finally came to a stop. It was a wide plateau with a large, flat area allowing a view of the surrounding hills and valleys. The views were magnificent and were totally unobstructed. As I looked down to the valley below, I felt as if I were standing on the top of the world.

I crouched out of sight and believe the apostles were unaware of my presence. I was sure Jesus knew I was there. He was always aware of everything around him and even knew other people's thoughts. Nothing ever seemed to surprise him, and he was never without an answer to the questions people asked, including questions intended to entrap him and cause him to violate the law. I didn't know why, but I was happy He allowed me to be there.

Suddenly, Jesus was changed. His face was as bright as the sun. His clothes became dazzling white, white as light.

And then Moses and Elijah appeared, and they began talking to Jesus as if having a normal daily conversation.

Peter said to Jesus, "Lord, it is good for us to be here. If you wish, I will build you three shelters— one for you, one for Moses, and one for Elijah." It seemed Peter wanted to be part of the conversation, and I'm sure he wanted the amazing experience to continue.

While he was still speaking, a bright cloud enveloped them. At that point, I couldn't see what was going on. So I took a few steps closer, trying to hear.

Then the voice of God the Father came from above. It was the same voice I had heard at the Jordan River, when Jesus was baptized. It was also the same voice I heard on the Other Side in my vision.

Then I realized I was not only in the presence of Jesus the Son, Moses, and Elijah, but now even the Heavenly Father himself had joined the group. I fell on my face and covered my head. I lay motionless like a dead man for fear I might be violating a holy moment.

Then the Father said, "This is my Son, whom I love. With him I am well pleased. Listen to him." This was the holy instruction meant for Peter, James, and John. God's instruction was to be quiet and listen.

I was still frozen on the ground, unable to move. I was even afraid to take a breath. Then I heard Jesus say, "Get up. Don't be afraid."

By this time, the cloud had cleared, and I saw the apostles getting up off the ground, where they also were lying in fear. I remained frozen to the ground like a fallen tree. Then I heard Jesus say, "I do not want you to tell anyone what you have seen here today until I have been raised from the dead."

After saying this, Jesus turned and again he looked directly at me. This time he was not smiling.

The combination of his words to the apostles and his look in my direction made it clear to everyone that he wouldn't tolerate any violation of his instructions. I'm sure no one wanted to know what the penalty might be.

The next day, Jesus sent the entire group of followers to Capernaum for a few days of rest. Both Matthew and I were looking forward to discussing the many things Matthew had seen and heard in the private teaching sessions the apostles had experienced with Jesus.

The holy moment I had experienced on the mountainside was a secret I would never reveal to anyone until the Resurrection. Not even Matthew.

The day after our arrival, the religious leaders came looking for Jesus, with another plan to trap him. The religious leaders knew people hated tax collectors, and they were angry about the abusive taxes the Romans had levied against them. They also knew Jesus had spent time with tax collectors during his ministry.

The plan was to come to Jesus with a question they believed would result in either the people turning against him or the Roman guards arresting him. This time they thought they had a question Jesus would be unable to answer without being trapped.

Satan and his demons had inspired the plan, come up with the question, and put it in the minds of the leaders.

They brought two Roman soldiers with them, promising to prove that Jesus was speaking out against the Roman government. They were certain Jesus would answer their question in a way that would result in an arrest. The soldiers stood by, ready to take him into custody immediately if he spoke against taxation. The leaders approached Jesus and asked, "Do you believe we should pay taxes imposed by the Roman government?"

As I heard the question, I realized it could not be answered without serious consequences. If he said yes, the people would turn against him. If he said no, the Romans would have him arrested for violating their tax laws.

Jesus didn't hesitate. He asked for a Roman coin. He held it up so everyone could see it, and he asked, "Who is the likeness on the front of this coin?"

They responded, "Caesar's."

Then calmly he said, "Give to Caesar what belongs to Caesar, and give to God what belongs to God."

The plan had failed. Once again, another defeat for Satan and the evil religious leaders.

The Roman soldiers looked at the leaders in disgust. "Why have you wasted our time?" And they walked away, obviously angry with the religious leaders and their false accusations.

A few days later, Jesus went to the Temple. A large crowd followed and sat down, waiting for him to teach. All of a sudden, there was a lot of commotion. The Pharisees and several other followers were dragging a screaming woman who had been bound and beaten. The Pharisees brought her to Jesus and said, "This married woman has been caught in adultery. Moses' law requires we stone her. What would you do with her?"

Once again, the religious leaders thought they had him tricked. They knew he was compassionate, and they hoped he would go against the Law of Moses so they could accuse him.

Jesus looked at the crowd and said, "What this woman has done is wrong. Her actions have damaged her relationship with her husband and set a bad example for her children. Regardless of her reason for her sin, her actions are unacceptable and have broken fellowship with her family and with God. The religious leaders tell you that you are responsible to keep the law in order to be righteous in God's eyes. I tell you keeping the law is impossible. Even if you never commit physical adultery but you lust in your heart, you have already committed adultery. If you never commit murder but you have hated your brother, you have committed murder in your heart. Even if you are able to fool every person in this town, remember that God knows your heart. He cannot be deceived."

Then Jesus bent down and wrote in the dirt with his finger. Only those closest to Jesus could see what he was writing. Then he said, "Those of you who have not sinned, cast the first stone."

One by one, they moved to the front and saw what he was writing. Then, one by one, they walked away, not looking back.

Jesus then looked at the woman and said, "Where are those who condemn you? Is no one left?"

She said, "There is no one left."

"Neither do I condemn you. Ask God to forgive this sin." Jesus gently helped her to her feet. "Remain faithful to your husband and sin no more."

As she walked away, the apostles came to Jesus and asked, "Should this woman's husband divorce her?"

Jesus said, "God, who created people in his own image, created them male and female. His plan is for a man to leave his family and be joined with his wife. The two become one flesh, so they are no longer two, but one. Whatever God has joined, no one should separate."

Then they asked, "Then why did Moses allow divorce and permit a man to send his wife away?"

"Because of the hardness of your hearts. Moses permitted divorce. I say to you, whoever divorces his wife and marries another commits adultery, except in cases of immorality."

They responded, "So in this case, the husband may divorce his wife because of her sin?"

"According to Moses' law, he may. But do you remember when I talked to you about praying?"

They said, "Yes."

Jesus said, "Then please repeat the prayer I taught you."

They prayed, "Our Father, who art in heaven, hallowed be thy name. Thy kingdom come, thy will be done on earth as it is in heaven. Give us this day our daily bread, and forgive us our sins, as we forgive others."

And Jesus said, "Stop right there. 'Forgive us our sins as we forgive others.' Have you sinned against your Father?"

Unable to continue to meet his gaze, they nodded. "Yes."

"Then you have your answer. If you want your Heavenly Father to forgive the sins you have committed against him, then you must forgive others."

Peter spoke up. "How many times must we forgive those who have sinned against us? Is there a limit, like five or seven?"

"Seven times seventy."

They looked puzzled. "That's every time, forever," one man said.

"Do you not know about Hosea and his wife, Gomer? God called Hosea to marry Gomer, a prostitute. Hosea was to have children with Gomer and make a home with her. After he did these things, she abandoned him and the children, yet God told Hosea to go after her, redeem her, and bring her home. In spite of the things Gomer had done, God wanted Hosea to reinstate her as his wife and the mother of their children."

Then the man said, "I'm not sure I could do that if my wife committed adultery."

Jesus clearly knew they were all thinking the same thing. "How long do I have to be with you? Can't you see that this story mirrors your own lives?"

They looked at each other, and they were still confused.

"Does that mean my wife is committing adultery?"

Then Jesus said, "You are all like Gomer when you live in a way that discredits God. When you choose to make anything in your life more important than God, when you love anything in the world more than God, when you do any of these things, you are doing far worse than Gomer did to Hosea. Listen to God's instructions to Hosea and apply them in your lives. So now, as I instructed this woman to go and sin no more, seek God with all your heart, and when the evil one comes with his temptation, flee from it. And when you see others failing just as you have done yourself, lovingly encourage them to seek God with all their heart. Be encouragers and edifiers, not condemners. Take time to share with them what God has done in your life, and seek to see their lives restored."

Some of them walked away, thinking this was too hard, their pride and their self-righteous, hard hearts preventing them from understanding the truth. They could not see how their sin had offended and grieved God.

To those who remained to hear further truth, Jesus went on, "Do not judge, or you will be judged. Be careful, because the same measure you use to judge others will be applied to you. Why do you look at the speck of sawdust in the eyes of others and pay no attention to the log in your own? How can you say, 'Let me take the speck out of your eye', when all the while, the log in your eye is blocking your vision. First take the log out of your own eye, and then you will be able to see clearly and remove the speck from the eyes of others."

As I listened, I realized I clearly understood this teaching. I thought about the times I'd judged others and told them to change while disregarding my own sin. This teaching touched my heart in a special way. It was truly convicting. I thought about the kind of husband and father I had been. How could I be so cruel?

Then Jesus said, "Remember God is love. He demonstrated his love through the forgiveness of sin for those who seek him with all their heart. Ask forgiveness and truly repent. God will hear your prayer. Do these things likewise when people sin against you. It gives God no glory when you love only those who love you. Anyone is capable of that, including those who do not believe. I tell you to love those who hate you, especially those who hate you because of your love for me. Then you will demonstrate you are truly one of my disciples."

Because he knew our hearts and minds, he added, "You think you can't possibly achieve these things, and you're right. Apart from God and his Spirit, it is impossible. But with God, all things are possible."

Jesus' wisdom and truth were molding and shaping us all. I realized nothing I could say was as important as the words the Son of God spoke. I knew Jesus had been sent by the Father as a messenger for the whole world, and now I saw that I needed to set aside my own agenda and just learn and apply these lessons.

Chapter Twelve

The next day, Jesus continued to teach about forgiveness. This time, I moved as close to him as I could.

"A man had two sons," Jesus said. "The younger one said to the father, 'Give me my share of the estate.' So the father divided the property and gave him his share. Not long after that, the younger son took his possessions and fortune and set off for a distant country. There he squandered his wealth in wild living. After he had spent everything, hardship and famine came upon the whole land. He hired himself out as a servant, taking care of pigs. He was so hungry, he wanted to eat the pods he fed to the pigs, but the owner would not give him even a few of them.

"When he came to his senses, he said, 'Many of my father's workers and servants have food to spare, and here I am, starving to death.' He thought about it, and he said, 'I'm going back to my father and say to him, "Father, I have sinned against you and heaven above. I am no longer worthy to be called your son. I'd like to work for you as a hired hand."' The next morning he left to go to his father and ask for forgiveness and a job.

From a far distance, his father saw him, and he was filled with compassion for his son. He ran to him, threw his arms around him, and kissed him.

The son said, 'Father, I have sinned against heaven and against you. I am no longer worthy to be called your son.'

"The father didn't respond the way the son had expected. Instead, the father said to the servants, 'Quickly! Bring my best robe and put it on my son.' He put a ring on his finger and sandals on his feet. Then the father said, 'Bring a fattened calf and kill it. Let's have a feast and celebrate, for this son of mine who was dead is alive again. He was lost but now he's found.'"

Then Jesus went on to explain. "The father represents God, our Father in heaven. The son represents those who have walked away from God to pursue the pleasures of the world. Many people, like his son, have yielded to the temptation of Satan. God has allowed all people to choose which path they will follow. When people choose Satan's plan, they reject God and his plan.

"The son had many so-called friends who were happy to help him squander his inheritance, but when the money was gone, he found himself alone and without a place to stay or anything to eat.

"One night, as he lay with the pigs in the pen, he thought about all the bad choices he had made, and he realized if he went to his father and asked forgiveness, his father would provide the things he needed to survive. His inheritance was gone, but in his father's house, the servants had a better life than the life he had chosen.

"Like the father of the wayward son, God waits for all people who have turned their backs on him and gone astray. He does not desire to condemn or punish them. He wants to restore the relationship that was broken, and he looks forward to the fellowship they were created to enjoy. Hear these words and accept your Father's invitation before the opportunity escapes you. Come home before it's too late."

By this time, it was late in the afternoon, but no one wanted to go home. One minute Jesus was teaching, the next minute he was healing. He seemed tireless. He never stopped working. He asked the crowd to sit down and listen to one more teaching before he retired for the evening.

Once again, I was in the front, eagerly listening and longing to learn more.

Jesus looked directly at me and said, "A rich man dressed in fine clothing and lived in luxury his whole life. At the gate of his home lay a beggar named Lazarus, covered with sores and longing to eat whatever fell from the rich man's table. Lazarus' poverty was so great, even the dogs in town had better lives than he did. At least they had shelter in harsh weather and were fed scraps from their masters' table."

Immediately I thought of a man just like this one, who stayed just outside my gate. He was a constant embarrassment. I never knew his name, but I always sent him away, only to find he had returned the next day. I had never considered that the beggar at my gate might not have a place to live. I saw him as a pest.

Jesus went on, "In time, the beggar died, and the angels carried him to Abraham's side."

I remembered the day my beggar died. He seemed to have fallen asleep, leaning against my gate.

Then Jesus said, "The rich man also died and was buried in hell, where there was torment. He looked over across the wide and deep chasm separating hell from Paradise and saw Abraham, far away, with Lazarus by his side. So the rich man called out in a loud voice, 'Abraham, have pity on me and send Lazarus to dip the tip of his finger in the water to cool my tongue, because I am in agony.'"

Then I realized the rich man in this story was me.

It was exactly what happened in my vision—and in my life. A cold fear shook me, as intense as my fear of the Other Side. I drew a deep breath and assured myself it was just a vision. It didn't mean I was going back to the Other Side, even though that's where the rich man in Jesus' story was. Just a vision. Just a vision ...

Jesus went on. "But Abraham replied, 'Son, you remember in your lifetime, you received the good things, and Lazarus received the bad things. But now he is being comforted here, while you are in agony. And besides, this great chasm between us prevents anyone from going across. The purpose of the deep canyon is to keep those who belong on the Other Side from coming here to the side of Paradise. No one can cross over from one side to the other."

Jesus continued and finished the story of the rich man. Then the crowd dispersed, but I felt paralyzed. How did Jesus know the exact details? But the answer was obvious. He must have been there.

The rich man in the story was a permanent resident of the Other Side, and he had no hope of ever leaving. This was not the future I wanted.

As I thought back to my visions of the Other Side, I could not forget the voice I heard. It was God's voice. Since Jesus told the story exactly as it happened, I realized that either the Father had told him the story or Jesus was there himself. But how could that be?

How could Jesus have been both here on earth and talking to the Father on the Other Side at the same time? Then I answered my own question: Jesus is the Son of God, and he's capable of things we humans do not understand. He doesn't have the limitations we have. Trying to understand God is like an earthworm trying to understand a human.

Suddenly, my thoughts were interrupted by the heat of the day. I realized everyone had left except my cousin Matthew, who was sitting under a tree, enjoying the shade.

I walked over and joined him. "How long have you been sitting here?"

"About twenty minutes."

"Why didn't you say something when the others left?"

"I thought God was dealing with you, and I didn't want to interrupt."

"I don't know how to explain this," I said, "but that last teaching ... that was me."

Matthew's eyes grew sober and he hesitated. "The man in the story sure did sound like you. He could have been either one of us. But Jesus is changing us. If we follow him, he'll lead us to eternal life, and it won't be a horrid place like the place that poor soul, the rich man, chose."

I did not choose that place. But I kept the thought and my anger to myself, not wanting Matthew to know how much it bothered me.

After several moments, I had composed myself. "You don't understand. That story happened to me. Remember when I told you I had been attacked by robbers? While I was unconscious, I had a vision. The events in the story happened to me, exactly as Jesus described. I was that rich man. God gave me another chance, and I want to convince everyone to change their way of life. If they don't, they'll end up in the same place God revealed to me. It was called the Other Side, just like in the story. No one would want to be there. If people could see what

I saw, everyone would listen to Jesus and follow his teaching. Nothing on earth is worth one day in that wretched place. That's why John the Baptist and Jesus are warning people."

Matthew gave me that older-cousin look I remembered from our youth. "Okay, God gave you this vision so you could convince people to change their lifestyle so they wouldn't go to hell. How many people have you convinced?"

I dropped my head in shame. "None."

"I thought so. I'm beginning to understand that, no matter what we say to people, only God can change their hearts. Of course, they also have a choice. They must accept the truth, obey God, and love him with all their heart. They must also accept the free gift of God's grace. You would think anyone in their right mind would accept that gift, because nothing has greater value than eternal life in heaven. Has anything Jesus said been a lie?"

"Of course not."

"Then why doesn't everyone accept what he says and follow him?"

I didn't have an answer.

"What about you? If you hadn't had that vision, would you be here today?" Matthew looked away as if he thought he might have been too hard on me. Then he gentled his voice. "I thought the world would bring me more joy in life. I wanted to be in control, to make my own decisions. I chose a cheap substitute over the truth, peace, and joy God has to offer. But now I know it's not just about choices. It's also about surrendering to God's control. But I doubt that even this message will help you convince anyone to change their life."

He didn't understand. He wasn't the one who'd had the vision. "It doesn't matter. I have to try. Reaching people who are just as lost as I was has become the most important goal in my life. I have to have God's favor."

A few days later, a messenger came to Jesus with word that his friend Lazarus was sick and dying. The man's sisters, Mary and Martha, wanted Jesus to come to Bethany, their home, and heal their brother before it was too late.

When Jesus heard the news, he said, "This sickness will not end in death. This illness will be used for God's glory so God's Son may be glorified through it also." His response seemed strange to everyone who heard it, but no one expressed their confusion.

Jesus loved Lazarus and his two sisters. But for some reason, he did not leave for another two days. The next day, he told his followers that

Lazarus had fallen asleep. What he meant was he had died. "But I will go and wake him up."

Still not understanding Jesus, the apostles said, "Lord, if he sleeps, he will get better."

So Jesus told them plainly, "Lazarus is dead, and for your sake, I'm glad I was not there so you may believe. But let us go to him." It seemed like a cold response from one who loved Lazarus, but we gathered our supplies and left together for Bethany.

When we arrived, Lazarus had already been placed in a tomb, and the tomb was sealed. He had been there four days.

Mary went out to meet Jesus when she heard he was coming. It was obvious she was still grieving and a little angry. "Lord, if you had been here, our brother would not have died."

What she was really trying to say was, "Why did you take so long to get here, especially when you knew he was dying?"

Instead, she said, "If you had come when you received my message, I know God would have given you anything you asked."

But Jesus said, "Mary, I am the Resurrection and the Life. Anyone who believes in me will live again, even though they die. Whoever lives and believes in me will never die. Do you believe this?"

"Yes, Lord, I believe you are the Christ, the Son of God, who has come into this world," Mary said. "I believe when I die, I will live again."

Then Martha also came running and fell to his feet. "If you had been here, Lord, my brother would not be dead."

When Jesus saw her weeping, he felt her grief. He was deeply moved in his spirit. He asked, "Where have they laid him?"

They replied, "Come and see."

When Jesus arrived at the tomb, he wept.

Some of the people said, "Jesus really loved Lazarus." Another man said, "If he could heal the eyes of the blind, he could have healed Lazarus."

Jesus went up to the stone placed across the tomb's entrance to seal it. "Take the stone away."

"But, Lord," Martha said, "Lazarus has been in the tomb for four days. His body will smell, as it has started to decay."

But Jesus said, "Did I not tell you that if you believe, you would see the glory of God? So I tell you, roll the stone away and open the grave." Jesus then looked up and said, "Father, I thank you, for you have heard me, and I know you always hear me. But I said this for the benefit of the people standing here, so they will believe you sent me."

When he finished, Jesus called in a loud voice, "Lazarus, come out!"

The crowd watched but didn't believe anything could happen.

Suddenly, Lazarus appeared. His hands and feet were wrapped in strips of linen. He had cloth around his face.

Jesus said, "Take off the grave clothes and let him go."

When Mary and Martha and all those around had witnessed the event and realized God had responded to Jesus' request and raised Lazarus from the dead, they all began to praise God. They were so happy, they called for a celebration of God's faithfulness, and they took time to praise him and worship him.

When the time of rejoicing was over, everyone went to Martha and Mary's home and celebrated for two days. There was singing, eating, and dancing—a joyful time for the entire town. Lazarus gave all the glory to God for his revived life and required all those in attendance to honor Jesus, his good friend.

A few days later, after the celebration, Jesus and his followers went right back to work. The next morning, he was teaching. A young rich man approached Jesus, saying, "What good things must I do to inherit eternal life?"

Jesus said, "Do you know the Ten Commandments? Do not commit adultery, do not murder, do not steal, do not give false testimony, honor your father and mother."

The rich man said, "I have kept the commandments since I was a boy."

"There is one more thing you must do. Sell everything you have, and give everything to the poor. After you have done this, come and follow me."

When the rich man heard this, he became very distressed. He had accumulated great wealth and had extensive property holdings. The idea of parting with any of the things he had accumulated, especially things that gave him security and status, was out of the question.

Jesus then said, "How hard is it for a rich man to enter the kingdom of heaven? It's easier for a camel to go through the eye of a needle than for a rich man to enter the Kingdom of God."

While Jesus talked to the rich man, I listened intently. I could relate to this specific instruction, probably more than anyone else in the crowd could, because my former wealth far exceeded that of the young rich man. I knew everything Jesus had told him was true. Money had become a barrier between the man and God. He and I had both been consumed by the lust for wealth and power. These sins prevented us from having an intimate relationship with God.

As I learned more and more by listening to Jesus, I realized many of my decisions grieved God. I longed to understand the plan God has for everyone, and I hoped it wasn't too late.

Additionally, neither of us had ever given credit to God for his generosity and faithfulness. I knew this man's choices would ultimately lead to the emptiness I was experiencing. Ultimately, he was destined for the Other Side. I hoped his heart would change before that day occurred.

Maybe I could relate to this man. Certainly, I felt moved to try. I stepped close to him and touched his arm. "I know the teaching of Jesus is hard, but I can assure you what he says is true. If you want eternal life, you must listen and apply the things he teaches to your life."

The rich man backed away and said, "Take your hands off me. What would you know about me or the cost of following him? Look at yourself— the way you're dressed. You think you can relate to me? I've worked all my life to get what I have, and he asked me to throw it away."

"He doesn't want you to throw anything away. He sees your heart, as I do. You and I have made the same wrong decisions. We made our possessions more important than our relationship with God. Until God is first in your heart, you'll never find what you seek. And you'll never receive the good things God wants us to have."

The man responded, "If his teaching makes you feel good, fine. I'm glad it works for you."

"It does, and it'll work for you too."

He shoved me away. "Step aside. I have an appointment."

I thought about what Jesus had said earlier, then I made one last attempt to reach this man. "What if you gain the wealth of the entire world, but you lose your soul? What good would it be to have that much wealth here and then spend eternity separated from God? On the day you stand before the Lord in judgment, you won't have any of these things you think are important today."

Then the rich man said, "I'll leave this matter for another day."

As he walked away, I was sad. I turned around and realized the whole crowd was watching and listening to our verbal exchange.

I looked at Jesus and once again saw the smile of approval, but no word. At least I had tried. But once again, I'd failed.

Then the men in the crowd cried out, "Then who can be saved?"

Jesus looked compassionately at the crowd. He knew they longed to understand. "The religious leaders would have you judge yourself by evaluating how well you keep their man-made rules and regulations. I tell you, do not look at each other. Look at Holy God. He is your standard. Follow me, embrace my teaching, and you will obtain and understand truth."

Realizing they still didn't understand, Jesus added, "Consider Abraham. He was not judged righteous by his lifestyle or the things he did for God. He was judged righteous because of his faith and obedience. Do likewise and receive the gift of eternal life. Never forget, this is a gift that is neither earned nor deserved. It is a gift offered through the grace of God."

Then Peter said, "We have left all we have to follow you."

"I tell you the truth," Jesus said. "Anyone who has walked away from the things of this world for my sake and the sake of the Kingdom of God will receive many times more than what they seek, both in this world and in the world to come. Accept me and my words and you accept the one who sent me."

Then Jesus took the Twelve aside. I moved close enough to listen again.

He said, "We're going to Jerusalem, and everything the prophets have written about me will be fulfilled. I will be handed over to the Romans. They will mock me, insult me, and spit on me. They will flog me and kill me. On the third day, I will rise again."

I didn't understand why Jesus would have to go through all this. After all, he had taught the truth. He healed everyone who asked for healing. He demonstrated unconditional love and forgiveness for everyone who came to him, looking for a better life. How could that be wrong?

I sensed I was running out of time to achieve the tasks God sent me to accomplish. So far, not one single person had changed from their old ways because of my efforts. I could not even claim to have led Matthew to Jesus. Certainly, he'd shown interest during our conversations, but realistically, nothing I had said had resulted in a change of his heart.

I had to admit Matthew's conversion was truly a miracle from God and not from my efforts. So what now? What would my future be? I believed I knew the answer to that question, and it struck terror in my heart. If only there was a way to escape my own destiny, a way I could impress both God the Father and Jesus.

Then I remembered what Jesus had said: What is impossible with man is possible with God. I asked myself what this might mean to someone like me. Was I beyond God's help? Were my sins so great I was beyond forgiveness? What could I do? There was something missing in me. I knew it. I could feel it. Something prevented me from enjoying the joy and peace and assurance the others had. But what was it?

I must try harder. At any time, the Father might take me home—or should I say, to the Other Side. All I wanted to do was stop thinking about it and focus on what I was sent to do.

Chapter Thirteen

The next day, on the way to Jerusalem, Jesus was confronted by a group of ten people with leprosy. They stood a long distance away, calling out to Jesus, "Jesus, Master, have pity on us! We believe you are the Son of God, and if you will, we will be cleansed and restored."

Jesus went up to them and embraced each person. As he did, the lepers were healed and completely cleansed. Every limb, finger, and face was restored. This was a true miracle.

The lepers were so excited they ran away in different directions to tell their relatives and friends what had happened.

Later that evening, one of them, a Samaritan, came back and threw himself at the feet of Jesus, weeping and thanking him for healing him.

Then Jesus asked, "Weren't ten of you cleansed?"

Before the man could answer, Jesus said, "Where are the other nine? You're a foreigner, but you're the only one who came back to praise God for what he had done." There was dead silence in response to his questions. Then he said, "Rise and go. Your faith has made you well."

After he had sent him away, Jesus said, "Our Heavenly Father is the source of everything good. Praise and thanks and admiration should be on your lips at all times. But times like these, when he has demonstrated his mercy and grace in a special way, we must celebrate our relationship with him in an equally special way."

Then Jesus took time and gave thanks to the Lord. His prayer touched the hearts of everyone present.

A few days later, while Jesus was in Bethany, he stayed at the home of Simon the leper. Mary came with an alabaster jar of expensive perfume, and she poured it on Jesus' head while he reclined at the table.

But when the apostles saw this, they were indignant. "This perfume should have been sold and the money given to the poor."

Aware of this, Jesus said to them, "Why are you bothering this woman? She has done a beautiful thing for me. The poor will always be with you, but you will not always have me. When she poured the perfume on my body, she did it to prepare me for my burial. I tell you the truth: wherever this gospel is preached throughout the world, what she has done will also be told in her memory."

The next day, before we left Bethany, we spent time resting before the trip to Jerusalem. Jesus sent two apostles ahead to the next village. Before they left, he gave them specific instructions.

"When you enter the village ahead of you, you will find a colt tied to the rail. No one has ever ridden him. Untie the colt and bring it here to me. If anyone asks why you're untying the colt, simply tell them the Lord needs it."

While we were all waiting for the others to return with the colt, I was hungry, and I ran into town to get something to eat. As I entered the town, I saw my uncle, Bartimaeus, who was blind. He had always been an embarrassment to our family because he was the only family member who was unable to support himself. No one was willing to help him. So Bartimaeus had become a beggar, sleeping where he could at night and walking the streets and asking for alms during the day.

That day, when I saw Bartimaeus, I no longer felt embarrassed by him. Instead, I felt great compassion.

I called to him and we sat down together, and I shared with him the food I had purchased from a nearby vendor. I began to tell him about Jesus, that he was the Son of God and would be coming through town very soon. I told him he would hear the crowds as they were calling for Jesus because this is what happened everywhere we went. I knew it would be hard, even for a blind man, to miss what was going on.

I encouraged him to call out to Jesus when he passed by. I explained I had seen Jesus heal every disease and knew if he believed Jesus could heal him, he would have his sight restored.

Bartimaeus agreed and said he would find a place near the road, and when he heard the crowd, he would call out because he believed what I was telling him. The idea he might have his sight restored was thrilling. I hoped Jesus would hear him in the crowd. I wished I could point him out to Jesus, but I was still restricted from talking to him.

When I returned, I found people throwing their cloaks on the colt so Jesus could ride. As we proceeded down the road together, people along the road spread their outer garments along the path, creating a barrier between the hoof of the colt and the soil of the path.

The crowds grew as people ran toward Jesus, throwing their cloaks on the ground. Some people cut palm branches off the trees, waving them and calling out, "Hosanna! Hosanna in the highest!"

Everyone was praising God and thanking him for the miracles they had seen and heard about. Some also called out, "Blessed is the King who comes in the name of the Lord. Peace in heaven, and glory in the highest." It was one of the most amazing things I had ever seen. Jesus rode a donkey colt, not a white stallion, yet still the people proclaimed him to be royalty.

Some of the Pharisees rebuked the apostles and the people, but Jesus said, "I tell you, if the people are silent, the stones will cry out." And he continued on his approach to Jerusalem.

Along the way, a loud voice cried out, "Have mercy on me! Have mercy on me!"

It was Bartimaeus. He repeated his plea over and over. Many people were crying out to Jesus, but my uncle's voice got Jesus' attention.

Jesus got off the colt. The people were yelling at Bartimaeus to be quiet, but Jesus hushed them instead. Jesus heard something different in Bartimaeus' cries of desperation. I even heard it myself.

Then Jesus said, "Bring him to me."

Jesus spoke a quiet prayer over Bartimaeus, and he was given his sight back. And he went away, praising God.

Jesus simply remounted the colt and continued as if nothing special had happened. As the city came into view, Jesus stopped and looked over it, weeping. He knew Jerusalem's future, and he knew the future of Israel.

Jesus turned to those closest to him and said, "Despite the cries of 'Hosanna, glory to God in highest,' the time is near when I will be despised and rejected by those expressing their adoration this day. I have come with a message from my Father, but they will reject it. I offer them a message that will lead them to truth, to abundant life with the Father, who is always faithful. They seek truth, but their desire to be in control and their unwillingness to surrender to his will prevents them from enjoying life to its fullest."

As we entered Jerusalem, Jesus proceeded directly to the Temple. When he arrived, once again he found the Temple filled with moneychangers and merchants selling their animals for sacrifice.

Jesus turned to us and said, "It is written, my house will be a house of prayer. And once again, they have made it a den of thieves and robbers." After he said this, once again he drove them out.

After the Temple area was cleared, he sat down and began to teach.

Over the next few days, the crowds of people who came to see and hear Jesus grew larger and larger. The Pharisees did not know what to do because Jesus had become so popular with the people. So they simply attended the teachings, looking for an opportunity to challenge him and accuse him of violation of their man-made laws.

The people loved him. They knew he was sent from God. They believed he was Messiah. At any moment, they expected him to call down his army from heaven and drive out the Roman rulers and their army. Every day they stayed close to him, hoping they could witness the event firsthand.

As the week progressed, Jesus' main focus was teaching on love and peace and how to experience an intimate relationship with God the Father. He healed and taught people, but he didn't discuss rebellion against the Romans. The religious leaders worked behind the scene, trying to accuse Jesus of false teaching and hoping the people would rebel against him.

Knowing what the religious leaders were trying to do, he pointed out the false teaching of the Pharisees and their failure to follow the same rules they imposed on the people.

Jesus knew his time to teach the people was running out. On several occasions, he explained what he was about to go through, that the Holy Spirit would come after his departure. He told us the Holy Spirit would remind us ofs the things he had taught us.

The next day, he shared one more story he wanted us to remember after he was gone. "A man planted a vineyard. He put a wall around it, dug a pit for a winepress, and built a watchtower. Then he rented the vineyard to some farmers and went away on a journey. At the harvest time, he sent one of his servants to the tenants to collect some of the fruit from the vineyard. But they seized the servant, beat him, and sent him away empty-handed. So the landowner sent another servant. They clubbed this man on the head and treated him shamefully. So he sent a third one, and that one they killed. He sent many others; some of them were beaten, others were killed. He had only one person left to send: his one and only son, whom he loved greatly. The father thought they would respect his son because he was his blood. But when the son arrived, the tenants said to one another, 'This is the heir of this property. Come, let us kill him, and the inheritance will be ours.' So they took him and killed him and threw his body out of the vineyard.

"What then will the owner of the vineyard do? Will he come and kill the tenants and give the vineyard to others?"

There was no response.

"Haven't you read the scriptures? The stone the builders rejected has become the capstone."

While Jesus was teaching, I remembered I had to be especially careful in Jerusalem. I knew there was still a warrant out for my arrest, and I didn't want to have another experience like the last time I visited this city. I was being careful who I talked to and where I went. I attempted to get as close to Jesus as possible but stay lost in the crowd. My thoughts distracted me from the question and statement Jesus had made. Was he suggesting he is the rejected capstone? Because he was so popular, that didn't make sense.

The next day, the religious leaders came once again to Jesus with another question they hoped would trap him. They asked, "You have done many wonderful things beyond human understanding. But we want to know by what authority you do these things."

And Jesus responded, "I will also ask you a question. Tell me, when John the Baptist was alive and was baptizing people, did his ministry come from God or from men?"

They huddled together and asked one another, "How should we respond to this question?"

I was standing near enough to hear the discussion. They talked about some of the things John had taught, including that he was not the messiah but that the Messiah would follow him. John also was bold in his criticism of the hypocrisy of the religious leaders.

They realized if they said his ministry was from God, Jesus would say, "Then why do you not believe?" The people loved John, and they knew if they said his ministry was from man, the people would stone them. So they decided to answer, "We don't know where his ministry came from."

Jesus said, "Then neither shall I tell you by what authority I do these things." He turned to the crowd and said, "Beware of the teachers of the Law. They like to walk around in flowing robes and love to be greeted in the marketplace. They love to have important seats at the worship time and places of honor at banquets. They devour the assets of widows for a show of their lengthy prayers. The day will come for leaders like these, and their punishment will be more severe than you can imagine."

Jesus continued, "Watch out that you are not deceived. For many have come before me, and many will come after me, claiming to be sent by God. Some will even claim to be me. Do not follow them. I alone am the Way, the Truth, and the Life. No one can come to the Father except through me. I tell you these things so you will not be deceived. If anyone tries to teach you anything that conflicts with what I have taught you, you will know their teaching is a lie. There is one God, one Father, one Son, and one Holy Spirit. Together we are one.

"Some things about God cannot be explained or understood by you. The Father has sent me to explain all you need to know about eternal life. Follow me. I will lead you to the one who has sent me. When you focus on me, you will never be lost. I have come so you might have life and have it more abundantly, both here on earth and in life in heaven. If you choose to follow these spiritually blind leaders, they will lead you into a ditch and even worse places. Rejecting the truth, I tell you, will have unimaginable eternal consequences.

"Things may come that frighten you, but do not fear, for I am with you, and I will always be with you. I will never leave you nor forsake you. The Good Shepherd will never abandon his sheep. And, in fact, a good shepherd will lay down his life to demonstrate his love for his sheep. You will hear of wars and rumors of wars. These things must happen at the end. Nations will rise up against nations and kingdoms against kingdoms. There will be earthquakes and famines and pestilence in various places and fearful events and signs from heaven.

"But before all this happens, they will lay hands on you and persecute you. You will be brought before the government religious leaders, and many of you will be put in prison on account of my name. You will be able to use these times to tell your persecutors about me. Do not worry about what to say or how to defend yourself. I will give you the words and wisdom you will need any time that is necessary. You will find your adversaries will not be able to contradict what you say. You may even be betrayed by a friend or family member, and some of you may even be put to death. Many men will hate you because of me, but not a hair of your head will be damaged. By standing firm, you will gain life—eternal life in heaven with me.

"When Jerusalem is surrounded by armies, you will know the desolation is near. How dreadful it will be in those days. There will be signs in the sun and the moon and the stars. On earth, nations will be perplexed and in anguish. At that time, they will see me coming on a cloud—a cloud of power and of great glory. When these things begin to take place, stand up, lift your heads up because your redemption is drawing near. Heaven and earth will pass away, but my words will never pass away."

Someone asked Jesus, "When will these things happen?"

He responded, "Only the Father in heaven knows. He has sent me to tell you these things so none of you would perish. Once again, I tell you, do not follow the teachings of those who have a message in conflict with the things I have taught you. I am the final revelation of God's truth. If you do not place your faith and trust in me, you will perish."

Over the next few days, Jesus continued to teach at the Temple during the daytime and spent nights on a hill called the Mount of Olives. Each morning, the people were waiting at the Temple for him. They eagerly awaited every new teaching.

I sensed something big was going to happen soon. It seemed Jesus wanted to teach us every-thing at once, as if he was pouring himself out to those who were listening. Many lives were being changed as they embraced the things he taught, especially those of the apostles. In some cases, it seemed they were receiving last instructions.

Meanwhile, Satan and his demons were hard at work casting doubt, confusion, and fear into the hearts of those who listened to Jesus. They knew the human weaknesses shared by most of the people listening to Jesus: pride, arrogance, and unforgiveness, to name a few. Just as quickly as the seeds of truth were planted into the minds and hearts of the listener, the demons were there, attempting to snatch them up. Besides these activities, there was great focus on the main objectives.

First was Judas, one of the Twelve, who had been assigned the duty of treasurer of the ministry. Judas had already demonstrated he could not be trusted by stealing money devoted to the ministry and work of Jesus. He was disappointed Jesus had not used his power to destroy the Roman invaders. Occasionally he had voiced his disapproval, only to have Jesus rebuke him. Because Judas was so self-centered and prideful, he was unable to receive the rebuke from Jesus in a godly manner. He became angry, holding a grudge. When the time was right, Satan would enter Judas and take control of him. This plan would result in the greatest betrayal in human history.

Second was the high priest, Caiaphas. Caiaphas had also become a useful tool of Satan because of his thirst for power and his desire to control the people. Caiaphas was extremely greedy. He enjoyed the respect the position of high priest gave him. Caiaphas, of all the people, should have been able to clearly see Jesus of Nazareth was, without a doubt, the promised Messiah.

Caiaphas ignored the comments of other Pharisees who stated they believed Jesus had come from God. As high priest, he was required to know the Old Testament and its prophecies so he could show the people who the Messiah was when he arrived. Caiaphas should have been the one to confirm the identity of Jesus and make people aware that the prophecies had all been fulfilled in the life of Jesus.

Caiaphas, along with most of the religious leaders, was concerned that the coming of the Messiah would bring about a change in God's covenant with his people. God had promised his people a new covenant that would put an end to the old ways of sacrifice and rituals. This, of course, would change the religious leaders' control over the people. God wanted all his people, not just the priests, to have direct access to him.

On many occasions, Jesus made it clear he had not come to destroy the old law but to fulfill it. This made the religious leaders angry because in making the comments, he declared himself to be the Son of God.

Additionally, Jesus made it clear he had come to be the final sacrifice for all the sin in the world—the unblemished Lamb, perfect and sinless, the Good Shepherd who gave his life for the sheep. After Jesus, no further sacrifice would be required, as his death on the cross was sufficient for the payment of all sin of all the people—past, present, and future, of every nation in the world.

Jesus also promised direct access to the Father. No longer would people have to go through priests. People could go to and through him instead. Jesus made it clear when he declared, "I am the Way, the Truth, and the Life. No one comes to the Father but through me."

Instead of recognizing Jesus for who he was and joining in spreading the good news, the leaders chose to try to eliminate him and his ministry.

Satan knew Caiaphas believed he had the most to lose if Jesus was allowed to continue his ministry and the most to gain if he was eliminated. As a result, Caiaphas had become a willing pawn in Satan's plan. Anyone in their right mind would wonder why Caiaphas did not ask the same question Nicodemus had asked, "How can I receive eternal life?" The religious leaders were arrogant and believed they deserved eternal life, so their focus was on the present rather than the future.

After talking to Jesus, Nicodemus said, "How did I not know these things? Even after Jesus did all those miraculous signs in front of my eyes, I still would not believe him."

This spiritual blindness fulfilled the prophecy of Isaiah: Everywhere, the Lord has blinded their eyes and their hearts so they can see with their eyes and not know what their hearts cannot understand.

Third, Satan and the demons had done their very best to place fear in the hearts of the remaining eleven apostles. Satan believed if he could destroy Jesus and make the Eleven doubt, they would be incapable of carrying on his ministry when he was gone.

Repeatedly, Jesus had told the Twelve he would be arrested, flogged, and killed. There was no question the apostles were concerned that if Jesus should die, they would be left alone. They could not understand how Jesus could be raised from the dead, even though they had seen Jesus raise Lazarus from the dead after four days in the grave. But if Jesus were to die, who would raise him? Could he raise himself?

They were all afraid to ask Jesus these questions, as this would demonstrate their doubt and lack of faith. Jesus knew their hearts and knew their fears, so he constantly encouraged them, knowing they would, in time, understand and be used in mighty ways in his Kingdom. God would empower them with what they needed to accomplish the task. He had prepared them well.

Satan, of course, did not know or understand God's plan. He was only able to see their weaknesses. He spent a great deal of time trying to discourage them and put special emphasis on Peter. Jesus had already identified Peter as one of the new leaders. While Peter was strong in human terms, parts of his character made him weak and vulnerable, and those were the places Satan attacked the hardest.

Satan spent a great deal of time on the Romans in positions of authority in Israel. He knew they could use force to control the people if they tried to defend Jesus. The Romans were small in numbers compared to the entire population of Israel. They were always concerned about an uprising, and they were prepared to respond with force to any group or person they might perceive as making trouble. They too had been watching and listening to everything Jesus had been saying.

Many of those who had been attending the teachings that day had become followers of Jesus. As enthusiasm for Jesus grew, so did the Roman officials' concern. Even though nothing Jesus taught suggested violence, the Roman officials were poised to stifle any uprising, but they were also concerned about maintaining a favorable relationship with the religious leaders. They needed these leaders to help control the people.

Last, there were many uninformed fence-sitters. Some of them were paid protestors, available for hire by the religious leaders. Many of them were already enlisted in Satan's army and were simply waiting for their marching orders. Satan and his demons were relentless as they worked twenty-four hours a day, seven days a week, constantly attacking the spirits of everyone involved. They had implemented their master plan, and they believed that plan would bring a conclusion to Jesus' ministry. If Jesus could be defeated, Satan thought, he and his followers would once again have control without interference.

It was the evening of Passover. Everyone had plans to join their family for a traditional meal. It seemed the whole city of Jerusalem had a place to go except me. Since there was no resolution with my family, and Matthew was going to participate in the Passover meal with Jesus and the other apostles, I remained alone with no place to go.

Even though Jesus had not called my name, I was rarely very far from the man I had come to love and hold in the highest esteem. I had become one of his top students. Listening to him over the last three years, I had internalized hundreds of stories and could repeat most of them by memory. In spite of my commitment to Jesus' teachings, all this knowledge remained in my head and had not completely changed my heart.

The evening of Passover, I followed Jesus and the apostles to the building where they planned to enjoy the Passover meal. I found myself sitting outside the building. I was close enough that I could clearly hear the conversation going on inside. Everyone was singing praises to God, and I joined them in singing outside. I had learned some of their songs over these last three years of ministry. I was familiar with all of them, even if I didn't know all the words.

As the evening progressed, there were times when I couldn't hear what was going on, but I heard Jesus say something about someone who was going to betray him. I wasn't sure what he meant. A little while later, Judas came out of the building, stealthily looking both ways.

I was curious so I followed him to a discreet place, where I saw him meeting and talking with one of the religious leaders. After a short conversation, the leader handed Judas a small bag or purse. Judas opened it and poured out some coins into his hand. The silver reflected the moonlight, leaving no doubt in my mind he was receiving some kind of payment.

It couldn't have been a contribution to Jesus' ministry. If it was some kind of a payoff, what was it for? Whatever the reason he was talking to an enemy of Jesus, I knew it couldn't be good.

For some time now, I noticed Judas had been acting negative and saying rebellious things toward Jesus. Matthew had said Judas made comments to him too.

I wanted to get close enough to Matthew to tell him what was going on, or to tell Jesus himself, but I knew I couldn't violate God's order and speak to Jesus. I couldn't just walk into the private dinner. All I could do was look for an opportunity to tell Matthew.

So I returned to the building and sat outside, trying to hear what was going on above me. In the room, Jesus called Matthew aside and said, "Your cousin Demas is sitting in the yard. Take him some food and tell him the time is near when

I will speak to him. He will be by my side, then we will have time to talk."

So Matthew brought the food down to me and told me what Jesus had said. I hadn't eaten all day, so the food was a blessing. But I was so excited when I heard Matthew's words that I forgot to mention what I had seen.

It was hard to hear what was going on. Several conversations were taking place at the same time, which would not be unusual in this kind of a gathering. Then, all of a sudden, everyone became quiet. Jesus seemed to be calling the meeting to order.

He then said, "I have much to share with you in a short time. You must listen to all I have to tell you and remember the things I am about to show you. You are going to have this light only a little longer. Walk while you have the light because before long, darkness will overtake you. The man who walks in the dark does not know where he's going. Put your trust in the light while you have it, so you may become sons of light.

"When a person believes in me, he does not believe in me only, but in the one who sent me. When he looks at me, he sees the one who sent me. I and the Father are one. I do nothing apart from the Father. I join him where I see him already working. This you should also do. As for the person who hears my words and does not do them, I do not judge him, for I did not come to judge the world, but to save it. For there is a judge for those who reject me and do not accept my word. When someone rejects me, they also reject the one who sent me. That decision will have eternal consequences. I do not speak of my own accord, but my Father who sent me commanded me what to say and how to say it. I know His command leads to eternal life."

My curiosity got the best of me. I climbed up the side of the building and peeked through an opening.

Without saying another word, Jesus got up from the meal, took off his outer garment, and wrapped the towel around his waist.

He poured a basin of water and began to wash the feet of each apostle, one by one. Then he came to Peter.

Peter said, "Lord, you're not going to wash my feet."

Jesus replied, "You do not realize what I'm doing, but later, you will understand."

"No, Lord. Never will you wash my feet."

"Unless I wash your feet, you will have no part of me."

Peter said, "Then, Lord, not just my feet, but my hands and my head as well."

"You call me Teacher and Lord, and rightly so, for that is what I am. Now that your Lord and Teacher has washed your feet, you should wash one another's feet. I have set an example. You should do for others what I have done for you. I tell you the truth. No servant is greater than his master. Nor is the messenger greater than the one who sent it. Now you know these things, and you will be blessed if you do them.

"One of you who has shared this meal with me has betrayed me. I am telling you now, before it happens, so you will know I am the one foretold in Scripture. These things must happen in order to fulfill the prophecy about the Messiah. I am not referring to all of you. I know the one who has given in to Satan's temptation."

All the apostles looked at each other, saying, "It's not me. Who would do such a thing?"

Then Jesus said, "My children, once again I tell you, I will be with you only a little longer. You will look for me, so I will tell you now, where I am going, you cannot come. A new command I give you: love one another as I have loved you. By this, all men will know you are my disciples."

And Peter said, "Why can't we follow you now, Lord? I will lay down my life for you."

Jesus said, "You'll lay down your life for me? I tell you, before the rooster crows, you will disown me three times."

Then Jesus said, "Do not let your hearts be troubled. Trust in God. Trust also in me. In my Father's house, there are many mansions. If it were not so, I would have told you. I'm going to prepare a place for you. I promise to come back and take you to be with me, so you can be with me always. I long for the day when you can see where I came from and where I am going. The time will come when you will know the way."

Then Thomas spoke up and said, "We don't know where you're going. How can we know the way?"

And Jesus said, "I am the Way, the Truth, and the Life. No one comes to the Father or comes to the place where I dwell except through me. If you really knew me, you would know my Father, as well. From now on, you can say from your heart you know the Father, because you've seen me."

And Philip said, "Show us the Father."

"Don't you know me, Philip? Even after I've been with you so long? Anyone who has seen me has seen the Father. I and the Father are one. He is in me, and I am in him. If you do not believe me, at least believe the miracles I've performed. Anyone who has faith in me will do what I am doing. He will do even greater things than this. I will do whatever you ask in my Father's name so the Son may bring glory to the Father. You may ask me anything in my name, and I will do it. If you love me, you will obey me, and you will obey what I command. The day is coming soon when the world will no longer see me, but you will see me because I live in you and also will live in those who put their trust in me. I must die and be raised again to conquer death. Then you will know there is life after death. My resurrection will provide irrefutable evidence to you and the whole world.

"Remember these words I spoke to you. No servant is greater than his master. If they persecute me, they will persecute you also. They will treat you this way because of my name. They do not know the one who sent me. He who hates me, hates the Father as well. It is written in their law: 'They hated me without reason.' All of this I have told you so you won't go astray."

Then he took bread and broke it and gave a piece to each apostle, saying, "This is my body." Then he took the cup and gave thanks and offered it to them. They ate the bread, and they drank the cup.

And Jesus said, "This is the blood that will be poured out for the forgiveness of sin. I will not drink this fruit until I drink it with you in my Father's Kingdom. Whenever you gather together, do these things in remembrance of me and the things I've taught you. Remember, I will always be with you. I will never leave or forsake you."

After this, they sang a song, a final hymn, and then they went to the Mount of Olives.

Chapter Fourteen

A s they left the place of the Passover feast, I followed them to the Mount of Olives and to a special place called the Garden of Gethsemane. I heard Jesus tell the apostles to "sit there for a while, while I go and pray."

He took Peter, James, and John along with him. They were to keep watch while Jesus went off to pray. When he began to pray, he seemed deeply distressed and troubled. I heard him say, "My soul is overwhelmed with sorrow to the point of death." Then he came back to the three and asked them to keep watch while he went a little farther ahead to pray. He walked a distance, and then he fell to the ground and prayed.

I had followed closely behind and continued to follow Jesus until he stopped. I sat down in a place where I could see the three apostles and Jesus. When Jesus fell to the ground and began to pray, it appeared to me he was driven to his knees under the weight of what was to come: the cross and the burden of sin. He knew his blood was to be poured out for the benefit of all creation. Even though I understood what was happening, I didn't like it, and I was frustrated with the apostles. They were all good men, but they seemed oblivious.

Then I heard Jesus say, "Is it possible this hour should pass from me? I know everything is possible with you. If it's your will, take this cup from me. Yet not my will, but your will be done."

Then Jesus continued to pray silently. He spoke no words but the look on his face told me he was in agony.

By this time, I had stopped watching the apostles. I was totally focused on Jesus. It broke my heart to see him suffering this way. Then he got up and went back to where the apostles slept.

I heard Jesus say, "Peter, are you asleep? Could you not keep watch over me for one hour? Please, watch and pray so you will not fall into temptation. I know your spirit is willing, but your body is weak."

Once more, he returned to the spot and began to pray again. This time, the prayer of Jesus was even more intense. I could hear the anguish in his voice, although I was unable to understand his words.

I remembered Jesus said he was going to be killed and be raised from the dead. He was to pay the price of sin for all mankind. He said this over and over again, but for some reason, no one seemed to understand. I kept asking myself why I was the one to understand. The purpose of his death was also clear to me. I didn't like the plan, and the purpose still remained a mystery to me. I was certain Jesus had the power to prevent any harm from coming to himself. Because he kept describing what was going to happen, it seemed to me he should do something to prevent it. And how would they convict somebody who had done so much good? He taught nothing but the truth and had healed many. How could the things he accomplished be considered bad or deserving punishment?

Then I realized it had to do with the prophecies. He was sent from God the Father with a message of God's love. The Messiah's life events had been foretold thousands of years ago. The teachers of the law knew the prophets had described these events in detail. They knew the prophecies, and yet they plotted together to kill Jesus.

Jesus appeared willing to allow these things to happen in order to demonstrate God's love for his creation and to provide a way for everyone to have their sins forgiven.

I realized how unworthy I was to receive the love the Father was going to demonstrate. I could not believe Jesus was willing to pay the price for the things I had done throughout my life. I couldn't help but wonder whether I was excluded.

I looked at Jesus praying, crying out to the Father in a loud voice now. I got up. I couldn't stand it any longer. I had to comfort him. I began to rush toward him.

Then the Father's voice boomed in my ears. "You may not comfort my Son in any way. My Son understands the events that are about to happen. He has known this day was coming for a long time. I will be with him, and I will comfort him."

I stopped in my tracks and returned to my place of hiding. I looked back and saw all the apostles still sleeping. Never in my life had I felt so helpless, but all I could do was watch. I couldn't talk to him or try to wake the apostles. What could I do? I just wanted the whole experience to end.

For a moment, I thought it might be worth the price to pay if I could comfort him. I realized then that I had fallen in love with Jesus—not Jesus the man, but Jesus my Lord. I know God had a plan, but I still struggled not to interfere.

The temptation to go to him continued. It was unbearable. Maybe I should not have followed everyone to the Garden.

There was nothing more I could do, so I fell on my knees and began to pray as I had never prayed before. In the past, I had prayed for myself or asked God to change a negative situation in my life. This time, my prayer was different. I began to cry out to God to comfort Jesus. I was unable to find the words to express my deep pain for him.

I asked God to wake up the apostles. I asked for wisdom, I asked if there was anything I could do. I waited for God's voice, but it seemed the last thing he said was his last word.

I prayed God would take away my feelings of helplessness. I closed my eyes and stopped my ears, trying to drown out what I was seeing and hearing. Then I began to pray for strength and courage. While I was praying, God began to reveal things that had occurred in my lifetime, starting with the day I was climbing trees with Reuben.

We were competing as children do, to see who could climb the highest and largest tree. Reuben went higher and earned the title of champion for the day.

All the children pointed to Reuben, in awe of his climbing skills—and I was jealous. I wished he would fall. Then I would be the one who could climb the highest.

Then, without warning, the branch broke. I will never forget the sound of his body hitting the ground. There was a loud thud followed by screams of agony. And he was paralyzed—until later in life when Jesus healed him.

It became clear that God wanted to show me the wickedness of my selfishness and show me how early in my life it all began. In all those years, I never visited Reuben. How could I have been so selfish? We were best friends. If I had fallen, Reuben would have visited me. I was ashamed of myself.

That was just the beginning. God showed me many other selfish decisions I made over my lifetime.

I recalled the first time I saw Goldie—how beautiful she was. The moment I saw her, I knew I wanted her to be my wife. Then I remembered how I had treated her and the children over the years.

What kind of husband and father had I been? I was truly ashamed.

Over and over, I thought about the decisions I had made and how they'd affected those around me, including those whom I claimed to love and were my friends. They saw my success and called me amazing, but the sad part was that they tried to duplicate what I had accomplished. As God revealed my choices and motives, I realized that, regardless of the praise, I was a failure in every area of my life.

I paused in my prayer and opened my eyes. Jesus was still on his knees, praying to the Father.

I wished I was more like him. I thought of all I had learned by listening to him and how life could have been different if I had only known and applied the concepts I had recently learned.

I looked up to heaven and cried out to God, asking for forgiveness for the way I had lived and for the harm and injury I had caused other people.

Something happened in that moment. A lump came up from the pit of my stomach to my throat. All of a sudden, I was unable to speak. I lost control, and my tears flowed uncontrollably. It seemed as though all the evil was flowing out of me. I couldn't understand or explain it, but I wept and wept. The more I wept, the more I felt forgiven. One sin after another came to the surface of my thoughts. As they did, I confessed them, and I felt God grant me forgiveness. I kept saying over and over again, "I'm sorry, Lord." I realized my cries were loud and might alert Jesus to my presence, but it didn't seem to matter.

In the end, the tears continued to flow, but these were a new kind of tears. For the first time, I felt tears of joy. I knew God had forgiven me, and I sensed a kind of freedom, as if a burden had been removed. The slavery to sin was broken. I felt freer than I had at any other time in my life.

I was a new person. I got up and walked over and sat down again on a nearby rock, exhausted, still not understanding what had just happened, but feeling as if something inside me had truly changed.

I glanced back at Jesus and realized he was looking at me. Would this be the moment? Would he speak to me now?

Then all of a sudden, Jesus got up and walked back to where the apostles were sleeping. He woke them up and said, "Are you still sleeping and resting? Enough, the hour has come. Look, I am about to be betrayed and given into the hands of sinners. Get up. Here comes my betrayer."

As Jesus was speaking, Judas approached him, along with a group of religious leaders and Temple guards.

Jesus said, "Judas, are you betraying me with a kiss?" As he said this, I realized why Judas had met with the religious leader and why he had received the coins. Now we knew who the traitor was.

Immediately, the apostles came forward, swords drawn, to defend Jesus. Peter struck one of the Temple guards, cutting off his right ear.

Upon seeing this, I drew my sword. I had such a tight grip on the handle, my knuckles turned white. I wanted to join in protecting Jesus.

As I stepped forward to defend Him, I heard God's voice again saying, "You cannot defend my Son in any way. I will not tell you again."

I stopped in my tracks and threw my sword to the ground, tears of frustration welling up in my eyes.

I heard Jesus say, "Enough." Then he picked up the man's ear from the ground and touched the ear to his head, and he was completely healed.

Then Jesus said, "You think I'm the leader of a rebellion that you have to come to me with clubs and swords? Every day, I've been teaching in the Temple courts. You didn't say anything then. Now you come in the middle of the night, in complete darkness. You do in the darkness what you have no courage to do in the light of day."

They seized him and took him to the house of the high priest, Caiaphas.

While I followed the crowd at a safe distance, I saw the light of two torches coming toward me. The two men were Roman soldiers who were also looking for Jesus. When they came upon me, they put a torch into my face, and one of them said, "Demas, is that you?"

As my eyes adjusted to the torch light, I saw a young man, maybe in his late twenties or early thirties. His face looked familiar, but I wasn't sure who he was.

"Yes, my name is Demas." I responded without thinking, believing it might be a friend. He said he had met me one time at the home of his uncle. His uncle just happened to be the Roman official who had experienced a large financial loss as a result of my advice. He was the person I had intended to visit the day I was attacked and nearly killed during my trip to Jerusalem. And he was the one who filed a complaint against me, resulting in a warrant for my arrest by the Roman government.

He reminded me of this outstanding arrest warrant and said I had to face charges for the financial injuries I had caused his uncle. He said, "My uncle will be very glad to see you. He's been waiting a long time to see justice served. Your arrest means I will receive a great reward and possibly a promotion."

They bound my hands and we followed the other soldiers as they took Jesus toward the house of Caiaphas. It seemed both Jesus and I would be held in prison to await our trial and punishment.

As we approached the house of the high priest, all the apostles ran away except Peter. I could see him across the courtyard outside the home.

I know he noticed me. Although I hadn't spoken to him directly, he knew I was a member of the Outer Circle.

I met with Caiaphas, and then I was instructed to wait in the courtyard of his home. Peter was there too, positioning himself to hear what was going on inside.

While we were all standing there, three different people approached Peter, asking if he was one of Jesus' followers. On each occasion, Peter denied he even knew Jesus. He said he was just interested in seeing what was going on. But after the third said, "I'm sure you were with him," Peter said, "You are wrong. I do not know him."

As quickly as those words came out of Peter's mouth, there was a loud rooster crow, just as Jesus had predicted. Of course, Peter and I knew the significance of the rooster crow. None of the other people did.

I saw him lean over, clutching his stomach as if in pain. Then he began weeping, and he ran away.

Where I was standing, I could see what was going on inside. They blindfolded Jesus and began mocking and beating him. One man punched him in the face and said, "If you are a prophet, tell us who hit you." Then they all laughed. The punching continued. This was mild compared to what was to come.

There was nothing I could do. The guards had me under arrest, and I couldn't defend or comfort him, per the Father's instructions. At this point, I had completely surrendered to his instructions.

I wanted to close my ears so I couldn't hear, but the thumping of fists and clubs against his body was a sound I will never forget.

We remained outside, waiting to find out what the captain of the guard would do with both Jesus and me.

Then I saw Jesus being led out of Caiaphas' home. As the guards came together, one of them said, "What happened in there?"

Another guard said, "The man Jesus said he is the Son of God. He is guilty of blasphemy."

At that point, the whole crowd, including Jesus and me, were escorted to the home of Pilate. I guess my guards were simply interested in what would happen. Many people brought false charges against Jesus, claiming he had intended to over-throw the government and was corrupting the established moral value because he had associated with prostitutes and tax collectors. They claimed he had opposed paying taxes to Caesar, and they said he called himself the "King of the Jews."

Pilate asked him, "Are you the king of the Jews?"

Jesus said, "Yes. It is as you said."

After hearing all the accusations, Pilate said, "I find no fault in this man."

The religious leaders continued to insist Jesus was stirring up trouble everywhere he went.

Pilate asked Jesus more questions, and then he said, "There is nothing wrong with this man. He has done nothing that would justify arresting or punishing him."

Then someone mentioned Jesus was from Galilee, so Pilate sent him off to Herod, who hap-pened to be in Jerusalem at that time. Because Jesus was from Galilee, he was under Herod's jurisdiction.

Herod was glad to see Jesus because he was aware of the miracles he had performed. He asked Jesus many questions, but Jesus gave him no answers.

The religious leaders continued to make false accusations against Jesus in front of Herod. Again, Jesus said nothing to defend himself.

Herod became angry because Jesus wouldn't show him any miracles and wouldn't answer any of his questions, so he had his soldiers ridicule and mock Jesus, dressing him in an elegant robe. Then he sent him back to Pilate.

A large crowd witnessed the incident with Herod. I was still with that group of people, under arrest, so I was able to see everything.

Several of the Roman government leaders were in attendance, and they questioned Jesus as well. As the soldiers left with Jesus, they escorted both of us to the jail, which was basically a dungeon. There was no light, other than a couple of torches. There were no windows. There was no fresh air. It smelled horrible. I could hardly breathe.

When we arrived, I was placed in a large dungeon filled with bruised, bleeding people. Some of them were near death. The odor filling the air was a combination of urine, excrement, and death.

Jesus was taken to a different part of the jail, and I was turned over to the soldiers in charge of holding about twenty prisoners in the dungeon area.

It was so dark in the dungeon, it took a few minutes for my eyes to adjust. As I glanced around the room, I noticed two men cowering in the corner. They had strange looks on their faces, almost as if they were afraid, then I realized they were looking at me. As I walked closer, I recognized them as the two men who had attacked me outside Capernaum. At first, I wasn't sure what to do. Then I remembered what Jesus had taught about forgiveness. I decided to confront them.

As I crossed the room, they tried to hide behind each other as if their fear was escalating. It seemed they thought I was going to harm them in some way.

Then I said, "I'm Demas. But don't be afraid. I haven't forgotten what you did to me or the harm you meant to inflict on me. But God has used that day and everything I've gone through since then, and he's changed me and my whole life. I can assure you, you have nothing to fear from me."

With that, I walked back across the room and sat down, but I kept one eye on them all the time.

Chapter Fifteen

━━━━━━━━━━⟶⟨⟩⟵━━━━━━━━━━

As the day progressed, news traveled throughout the jail, and it wasn't long before we heard Jesus had been formally arrested and tried by Pilate and Herod. He'd been found not guilty.

In spite of this, the religious leaders demanded his execution.

In the background, we heard the sounds of flogging and torture. We weren't positive it was Jesus, but the other prisoners said it wasn't anyone from their holding area. We could hear the guards laughing and cracking their whips and the screams of anguish.

Pilate's original plan was to punish Jesus and then release him, but after he announced his decision, the religious leaders rallied the people to protest Pilate's decision.

Finally, Pilate agreed to a more severe punishment. He asked the people what should be done. At the encouragement of the religious leaders, they screamed, "Crucify him!" over and over again.

"What crime has he committed?" Pilate asked.

They continued to yell, "Crucify him!"

Everyone in the jail could hear the screams, and they sent chills down our spines. The crowd was out for blood. We were fearful they might call for all of us to be crucified too.

Finally, Pilate walked over to a basin of water and washed his hands and said, "I have washed my hands. I am innocent of the punishment Jesus is about to receive. I find no crime in the man's actions. His blood is on your hands."

All the people answered, "Let his blood be on us and our children!"

With that, the guards led him away and continued to beat and flog him. The beating was so severe, the bones in his spine were exposed. His beard was pulled out by the roots. His face was beaten to the point no one could recognize him except his family members.

While this was going on, I noticed a young man sitting in the corner. I introduced myself and discovered his name was Amere. He appeared frightened and tired. I approached him, began to talk and found out Amere had a wife and two children, a boy and a girl. He had no money and no job. His family was so hungry, he stole some food from a wealthy Roman citizen. Theft was a crime in the Jewish community, but theft from a Roman citizen brought a harsher penalty. He was awaiting trial. The Roman courts enjoyed making an example of anyone who committed a crime against a Roman citizen. Amere might never see his family again.

As I talked to him, I began to wonder how Goldie and the children were doing.

Over the next hour, I tried to encourage Amere. Our conversation was interrupted by the loud mocking of Jesus and the noise created by their beating and swearing.

Neither Amere nor I knew what kind of punishment we would receive, but we expected a long prison sentence and possibly death.

We were both remorseful about the things we had done during our lives and the consequences of bad decisions. I encouraged Amere to ask God for forgiveness and trust Him with his future.

I told him God is love. I explained I was sorry about the consequences of my sin, but as time has gone on, I understand my sins separated me from God, and that grieved my heart. I was sorry for what I had done over the years, not only to other people, but to my family. I believed God had forgiven me.

"Amere, if you are sorry, ask forgiveness and do everything in your power to avoid the sin again. God will help you and give you the strength to flee from sin."

All of a sudden, the cell doors flew open and six guards entered, three with swords drawn and three with spears. They appeared ready for either combat or punishment. Behind them followed the commanding officer of the jail. He told everyone to stand up and line up against the wall.

Amere motioned to me to follow him and do exactly what I saw him do. He had been through this exercise before, he whispered, and he knew the penalty for not following orders.

We all lined up against the wall, looking at the floor so no one would have eye contact with the guards. Sometimes, the guards thrust a spear or slashed a sword at anyone who appeared to be challenging one of the guards' instructions.

A roll call was given. Amere whispered, "Just say 'here.' Don't look up. Don't look at anyone. If you do, they will hurt you."

After the roll call, the commanding officer said to one of the prisoners, "Barabbas, step forward."

Barabbas had been convicted of crimes against Rome and was awaiting a death sentence. He had been the leader of a small band of rebels who encouraged others to rise up against the Roman invaders. Every day, he waited to hear his name called. He never knew what day he would receive his punishment. Each day at roll call, the soldiers looked at the prisoners and acted as though this was the day they would be executed. Many of the men collapsed in fear or urinated on themselves when they heard their name. The guards would laugh and say, "Not this time, but maybe next time." The guards took great pleasure in seeing and inflicting fear. If the prisoners stood up to the harassment, it got worse.

Today, the guard called Barabbas' name.

Barabbas stepped forward defiantly, as if his anger and bitterness toward the Romans over-ruled his fear of death.

There was silence for a moment, then the jailer said, "You should be on your knees, thanking God today. Our great and generous leader, Pilate, has chosen you to be released and has forgiven you for your crimes against Rome. You are to leave without punishment so you can spread the word to your fellow Jews about the fairness and benevolence of the great Roman government."

And they led him away.

Then the jailer raised his voice for all to hear and said, "You have just seen an example of the fairness of our government and how we demonstrate compassion, even against the worst offenders of the law. Now Pilate has decided to extend his generosity toward two more people. He has decided to allow two of you to be treated as kings for this day. Those who would like to take advantage of this generous offer, please step forward."

Amere whispered, "Do not volunteer. This is part of the game."

I took his advice and remained in line, looking at the floor.

The jailer continued, "Come on, now. Isn't there anyone who would like to leave this wretched place, even for one day? One whole day of royal treatment. Don't you want to see the light of day and feel the warmth of the sun and smell the fresh air?"

After no one stepped forward, the jailer became angry. He said, "You try my patience by refusing the generosity of Rome." And he said to the other jailers, "Take two of them—any two."

Then he said, "The two selected will spend time in the presence of the King of the Jews. In fact, you will be at his side for a long time." He laughed.

The two guards came down the line, taking the first man, who struggled, and then they selected Amere.

As they began to remove Amere, I said to the guard, "Please, sir, not this young man. Take me."

The guard smiled and said, "As you request."

And they took me and led me away with the other prisoner.

I wasn't sure what was about to occur, but I knew it wouldn't be pleasant. I had told Amere to ask forgiveness for his sins and repent for the things he had done wrong, not only the taking of the food, but other things he had done in his lifetime. I told him if he got out of prison, he should look for those who were teaching what Jesus had taught. They would help him and his family to understand the born-again experience and the generosity of God the Father. They would tell him about God's offer of eternal life and to live with God the Father forever.

As we left the prison, neither I nor the other prisoner knew what our fate would be. I had taken a liking to Amere, even in the short time we had been together. I didn't feel his offense was so great that he should go through whatever the Roman soldiers had intended.

The Romans didn't need much of an excuse to demonstrate their brutality. Those who had felt the whip believed the Romans looked forward to making examples of anyone who even slightly opposed them and their oppressive government. At the very least, I knew both of us would experience a severe beating or worse.

Moments later, our fate was revealed to us in a shocking way. We were led down a dark alley into the sunlight. Blinded by the light, our eyes slowly adjusted and revealed Jesus beaten beyond recognition, with a crown of thorns firmly planted on his scalp. Blood covered his body from head to toe. His condition caused both of us to stop in our tracks, gasping for a breath of air that didn't seem to come.

Then, when I did finally breathe in, I thought I was going to vomit. The sight of his beaten body drew our attention away from the large wooden cross leaning against his shoulders. Then we noticed two other crosses, waiting for our shoulders. All three crosses were newly fashioned, clean, with bare wood that would soon be stained with our own blood. Alon, the other prisoner, and I had witnessed others who had been executed in this gruesome way. Neither of us had ever believed we would experience it for ourselves.

Fear and shock ran through our bodies as we anticipated our crucifixions—what it would be like when nails would be driven into our hands and feet and the suffering would begin.

The Roman soldiers knew all Jews feared crucifixion, and the cross had become a useful intimidation tool that kept the citizens under control. Because of this fear, it was especially cruel that any Jew would call for the death of Jesus in this manner. Crucifixion was extremely painful, humiliating, long-suffering, and without doubt the worst way to die that had ever been devised by evil men. The religious leaders were sending a message to all of Jesus' followers. They were not going to tolerate anyone taking a stand against their rules and rituals. Their authority had been challenged, and they wanted to make sure it would not happen again.

Jesus, Alon, and I followed a path leading up to Golgotha, which means "place of the skull." It was also called Calvary. Golgotha was to be my final destination on earth—where my crucifixion would take place.

As we began to climb the hill, the combination of fear and anticipation became so severe, my legs collapsed and would not move. Suddenly, I felt the tip of the whip as it slashed my back.

It's hard to believe, but the pain was a welcome distraction because it momentarily took my mind off what was about to happen just a few hundred yards away.

When we finally reached the top of the hill, a large crowd was waiting for us. Many relatives, friends, and followers of Jesus were there, as well as the religious leaders who wanted to make sure the sentence would be carried out.

There were three holes in the ground. They were placed far enough apart so the three of us could be displayed in an upright position after being nailed to our crosses. Jesus was first to be nailed. There was no struggle on his part. He simply gave himself up, not resisting in any way.

The guards had crucified many people. One said he had never seen anyone lie quietly and allow himself to be nailed to the cross this way. This was especially significant in the case of Jesus. Everyone knew Jesus was found not guilty by Pilot and Herod. An innocent man was being executed for a crime he did not commit, and still he didn't struggle or argue that he was innocent.

The second person to be nailed to the cross was Alon. Alon didn't make it easy for the guards. It took six men to subdue him, and they forced him to submit to the cross. They held him down and nailed his hands and feet in the same manner they had nailed the hands of Jesus.

I knew there was no way for me to escape. So I followed Jesus' example and surrendered to the cross. I lay down, extended my arms, and received the nails.

The pain was excruciating. Once the nailing began, my body seemed incapable of just lying there motionless. I tried, but my body instinctively fought back. I didn't understand how Jesus could go through this torture without responding.

After all three of us were nailed to the crosses, the guards lifted the crosses and dropped them into the waiting holes, placing the crosses in an upward position.

During the next few hours, Jesus' friends and relatives shed many tears, but others insulted him.

The religious leaders were angry because Pilate had placed a sign that said, "King of the Jews" over Jesus' head. They asked the soldiers to remove the sign, but the soldiers were under strict orders from Pilate to leave it there.

The insults continued. Some of those who had been mere spectators in the beginning became bolder and began to use vulgar language toward Jesus. Others attempted to spit on him. But one soldier, an officer, commanded his men to keep the people back and prevent them from spitting or touching those being crucified. He seemed to have respect and admiration for Jesus.

In spite of the darkness of this day, there was a bright moment. As I glanced across the crowd, my gaze fell upon Rahab, the prostitute from Capernaum. Rahab was weeping uncontrollably. When our eyes met, I realized someone had given her the message I'd tried to deliver to her about changing her life. And she had clearly received it. Her face glowed. She had been changed. Mary Magdalene and others sat nearby, consoling her.

As the day went on, the pain and the loss of ability to breathe was slowly taking its toll on the three of us. Exhaustion overtook our bodies, and we fell forward, making it difficult to breathe. The only way we could improve our breathing was to push up on the nails piercing our feet. The pain was excruciating, but our bodies continued to push involuntarily as we gasped for another breath, trying to survive for at least a few more seconds with each push.

The pushing continued in spite of the pain, almost as if the body was saying it needed to breathe. No conscious effort occurred. We didn't decide to push, it just happened automatically. Our lack of control over our own bodies made the torture even worse. It was as if our bodies became participants in administering the pain.

Up to this point, Jesus had not said a word to anyone. Ever since the moment I realized who he was, at the Jordan River, all I wanted was to be close to him. And now, here I was, as close as I'd ever been, but still unable to speak to him.

As I waited for some word from him, I sensed my time was running out. The temptation to say something, even knowing I would immediately be taken to the Other Side, was very strong. But I realized that even though this experience was unbearable, it would be better to remain here with Jesus and hang on the cross as long as I could rather than go to what I'd seen on the Other Side.

I thought back to the conditions I had seen on the Other Side. I wondered how things could have been if I had lived the way God wanted me to. I could have experienced eternal life in Paradise instead of the Other Side.

Grief came over me. If only I had known earlier what I knew now, my choices would have been different. I wouldn't have made so many bad decisions. I definitely would not have found myself hanging on this cross.

But at least I wasn't separated from God. I was right at his side at that moment.

Then it happened. I heard Jesus speak. "I am thirsty."

Someone filled a sponge with vinegar and offered it to him. He refused to drink. Then he looked at his mother and his best friend, John, who were standing together at the base of the cross. He said, "Mother, here is your son." Then looking at John, he said, "John, here is your mother."

John said, "I will take care of your mother."

Then Alon, the other thief, began to swear at Jesus. He snarled and said in a halting voice, "What kind of king are you? If you're the Son of God, call down your angels and have them remove us from these crosses. You're a fraud, a fake. You deserve the cross more than I do. You have blasphemed God. At least I admit I am a criminal, but you are a fraud."

I waited to hear how Jesus would respond. I knew who Jesus was and I was enraged by the thief's comments.

Jesus remained silent. He chose not to defend himself.

By this time, the crowd had become quieter. But there was an occasional outburst from Alon. Each time he expressed his anger, he directed all his comments at Jesus. This seemed to fuel the emotions of those who hated Jesus, and they joined in with their comments while encouraging Alon to "keep going."

Then Jesus spoke again. "Father, forgive them, for they know not what they do."

Then Alon said, "Don't ask God to forgive me. I mean every word I've said. You are a fraud."

With that comment, I broke my silence. I was unable to control myself any longer. "Alon, do you realize what you're saying? This man, Jesus, is the Son of God. He really is the King of the Jews, just as he said. Jesus has come to demonstrate the Father's love to all of us. He taught us to love, but we responded in hate. He healed every disease known to man. Because of Jesus, the blind see, the deaf hear, the lame walk. And those who were possessed by demons are free. Those who should know better have responded by flogging and crucifying the one and only Son of God. This is the worst example of pride and arrogance and selfishness in the history of the world. Alon, you and I deserve to be here. But Jesus is an innocent man. He hangs between us, not because he deserves to be here but because of false accusations made by the jealous religious leaders. They refuse to hear the truth and see the truth when it's standing right in front of them. How could they be so blind?"

There was silence everywhere, especially from the religious leaders. They were unable to refute the things I said because they knew it was the truth.

Then Jesus turned, looked at me, and said, "Demas."

I could not believe my ears. I thought I was hallucinating, so at first I didn't respond.

And then I heard again, "Demas."

When he said my name, it was a sound like I had never heard before. At that moment, nothing else mattered. It was a moment of intimacy with the Creator God. And it was all worth it.

"Yes, Lord?"

"You have learned much since you have been with me."

"Yes, Lord."

"I hear your words, but more importantly, I see your heart. Because of what you just said, you will be in Paradise with me today."

"But Lord, how can that be? I have failed in my assignment. I was given the opportunity to try to convince others to change their way of living, but I've done nothing to deserve being in your presence. I have failed."

Jesus said, "Oh, no. You have not failed. One person's heart has been changed."

"Who is that, Lord?"

"The one whose heart has been changed is you."

Then Jesus said, "Demas, you must understand. It is not what you have done to deserve Paradise, but what I have done here, this day. I have given my blood to cleanse those who have put their trust in me. My innocent blood has paid the price for every sin you have ever committed and for the sin of the whole world. Your only responsibility was to receive the free gift I offer. Is that your desire?"

I said, "Yes, of course, Lord." At this point, I realized Jesus and I were not communicating in the usual way. We seemed to be communicating one mind to another. So I asked him how I could understand what he was saying without hearing his words.

Then I heard him say, "Demas, I have much more to show you. I will explain these things as they happen."

I turned to Alon, and I tried to convince him to use the remaining part of his life to ask God's forgiveness for his sin and put his trust in Jesus.

Alon refused. His heart was hard, and he was bitter.

Shortly after our brief communication, Jesus looked toward the sky. He said, "Father, into your hands I commit my spirit." And he died.

About an hour after he died, the soldiers were ordered to break Alon's legs and mine. With broken legs, we would be unable to push up to breathe, to get whatever air we could take in.

Fear struck me as I thought about the pain I was about to experience. I knew the moment my heart stopped beating, I would know my fate. I understood what Jesus said about being in Paradise with him, but I was still confused because I had not been able to convince anyone to change their life. I didn't deserve the promise Jesus had made to me, but then I realized only a fool would reject it.

As I waited for the guards to come and break my legs, I heard the voice of the Father speak to my heart again. "Demas?"

And I said, "Yes, Father?"

"I am with you. I will never leave you. I will never forsake you."

"I'm afraid—afraid of the pain and the suffering."

"Remember the words David wrote when he said I would be with him through the valley of the shadow of death. And David said he would fear no evil. That's what I want for you, Demas. I want you to fear no evil because I will be with you. I will be right there with you. I will comfort you, and I will not leave you. And I will show you the way to Paradise."

And then I said, "You mean I'm going to Paradise, Father?"

"Yes, Demas. As Jesus told you, it's not about what you did or what you could accomplish. It's about what he accomplished today on the cross, as he paid for the sin of the world and demonstrated my love for each person, each one of my creation. This is not over. Soon Jesus will conquer death when he is raised from the dead."

After the Father finished speaking, out of the corner of my eye, I saw the Pharisees talking to the centurion. The Pharisees were all talking at the same time, and I couldn't understand what they were saying. They kept pointing at the three of us hanging on our crosses. It appeared they were making some kind of demand of the centurion.

He called some of the other soldiers together to discuss the demands, and then I saw the soldiers gathering tools of their trade.

Because I had seen a crucifixion once before, I knew what was coming next. As I helplessly hung on my cross, barely breathing, I wondered how this could be happening to me. I never dreamed I would be the victim of this kind of cruel punishment.

Next, one of the soldiers approached Jesus. I was certain he was already dead. For a long time, he had been hanging very still, making no effort to breathe. Both Alon and I continued to struggle for breath in spite of the excruciating pain each time we pushed down on our nailed feet. In spite of Jesus not making any effort to breathe, the soldier jabbed him in several places to see if there was a response. With one last thrust of the spear, the soldier pierced Jesus in the side. When he withdrew the spear, what appeared to be water came out of his side, then the soldier said, "This one is dead."

Next, I saw another soldier coming toward me with a club. I knew this was going to be the end.

The idea of the bone-breaking pain I was about to experience was terrifying. I tried to focus on the promise Jesus had made to me earlier. His promise gave me momentary peace.

Just before the blow came, I looked at Alon. His eyes were filled with terror. I closed my eyes, trying not to anticipate the blow and not thinking about the pain that was to come.

In a way, it was a blessing that I was first to have my legs broken. I was sure Alon was suffering as he thought about his turn. As for me, I just wanted the suffering to be over. I tried to focus on Jesus and the things he said. But my flesh demanded to survive, even if it was just for a few more seconds.

With one more push and a gasp for air, I used what voice I had left and said as loud as I could, "Jesus, don't forget me."

Then the blows came. First my right leg and then my left. The crucifixion had left me in shock. I didn't think my body could experience any more pain than it already had.

But the blows that broke my legs discovered nerves still alive and undamaged. The bone breaks took me to a new level of pain, a level I did not realize existed.

I momentarily hung motionless, then my body began to respond to the lack of oxygen. My muscles gave one more involuntary push against my broken legs in an attempt to breathe, but to no avail. By now, I had lost control over my own body, which made my torture even worse. My body had become my worst enemy as it struggled to breathe.

Then, the end. The end of my physical life and the end to all my pain. As life left me, I felt my body slump.

Instantly I found myself in the exact spot I had seen in my vision of

Paradise. To my left was the Great Canyon, and beyond the canyon was the Other Side. To my right was a beautiful garden with the Heavenly City in Paradise clearly visible.

Then I noticed Alon walking toward the canyon with Escort. I heard Alon say "But I don't want to go this way, I want to go toward the city with the light." The same words I used in my vision. I couldn't help but wonder how many times Escort had heard those words before.

I wanted to call out to Alon with some words of encouragement, but I restrained myself. It was too late. He had made his choice. For Alon, the time to have a change of heart had passed. His future and destiny were of his own choosing. Grief came over me as I knew the hopelessness and regret he was about to experience. I watched them fly across the canyon.

As I awaited my turn to be escorted, I again thought about what Jesus had promised. I had given a lot of thought to my condition and unworthiness. I knew my only hope of entering the Holy City was Jesus and the promise he made to me. Now I understand why he said, "No one comes to the Father except through me."

When Escort arrived, he had a troubled look on his face. I waited to hear the worst. I spoke first. "You look troubled. Are you okay?"

"This happens to me every time I take someone to the Other Side," he said. "Whenever I arrive, I hear cries of anguish and requests for mercy. I constantly have to remind myself that each person has made their own choice. I am simply delivering them to the destination they chose in their lifetime."

He continued, "Everyone on the Other Side has regrets for the decisions they made and the times they rejected the Father's attempts to reach them. Those thoughts and memories will never leave them. It's so sad."

Escort breathed in deeply and his face softened as he said, "The other part of my job brings me tears of joy as I escort some to the Heavenly City, the dwelling place of our Heavenly Father and His Son, our Lord Jesus."

As he spoke, my head went down. I knew my fate was about to be revealed. I focused on every word he spoke. Then there was a moment of silence.

I looked up and saw his eyes were filled with tears. Then he smiled at me and said, "Yes, Demas, you and I are going to see the Father. You are going home."

We both wept tears of joy as we began our journey to the Heavenly City. Each step we took brought us closer to the source of love, peace, and joy I had always been searching for.

Afterword

This story came to me in a vision. I believe God wanted me to tell this story to everyone seeking truth.

I asked God, "What should I say if someone asks me where this story came from?"

The Lord said, "Tell them I allowed you to see what happened through another's eyes."

If you enjoyed this story, I encourage you to explore the source of all truth, the Holy Bible, which is, of course, where most of this story came from.

CPSIA information can be obtained at www.ICGtesting.com
Printed in the USA
LVOW11s1209240714

395670LV00001B/1/P